PROFESSIONAL COMPETENCIES —TECHNOLOGY AND THE LIBRARIAN

Papers presented at the 1983 Clinic on Library Applications of Data Processing, April 24-26, 1983

Clinic on Library Applications
of Data Processing: 1983

Professional Competencies —Technology and the Librarian

Edited by
LINDA C. SMITH

Graduate School of Library and Information Science
University of Illinois at Urbana-Champaign

Library of Congress Cataloging in Publication Data
Clinic on Library Applications of Data Processing
        (20th : 1983 : University of Illinois at Urbana-
        Champaign)
        Professional competencies—technology and the
librarian.
        "Papers presented at the 1983 Clinic on
Library Applications of Data Processing, April 24-26,
1983"—Half-title p.
        Includes bibliographical references and index.
        1. Libraries—Automation—Congresses. 2. Library
science—Data Processing—Congresses. 3. Library
science—Technological innovations—Congresses. 4.
Library education—Congresses. I. Smith, Linda C. II.
University of Illinois at Urbana-Champaign. Graduate
School of Library and Information Science. III. Title.
Z678.9.A1C5   1983   025.3'028'54   84-6047
ISBN 0-87845-070-X

85-20

CONTENTS

INTRODUCTION

The twentieth annual Clinic on Library Applications of Data Processing was held April 24-26, 1983, at the Illini Union, University of Illinois at Urbana-Champaign. The Clinic theme emphasized the human side of library automation: professional competencies required to make effective use of new information technologies. The papers included in this volume consider how professional roles and responsibilities have been and are being affected by technological change and what competencies are important in filling these roles. In addition, approaches to training and education to develop competencies are explored.

In her paper presented as the keynote address of the conference, José-Marie Griffiths provides a framework from within which to consider the papers which follow. Describing progress on a study for the U.S. Department of Education to determine the present and future competencies needed by library and information professionals, she notes the need for communication among information service organizations (including libraries), professional societies, and education and training organizations. Competencies are defined as comprising one or more of the following components: knowledge, skills and attitudes.

New technologies are affecting activities in both technical and public services in all types of libraries. Kathryn Luther Henderson provides a detailed review of how technology is changing approaches to acquiring, organizing and preserving library materials, "the most typical of the activities of libraries." Drawing from a review of the literature, a survey of individuals working in technical services positions, and an analysis of position announcements, she considers competencies in two broad categories: (1) general, technical and bibliographic; and (2) managerial, supervisory and communicative. Danuta A. Nitecki also draws upon a review of the literature and an analysis of position announcements in her discussion of competencies required of public services librarians. In her view the competencies required—i.e., to communicate with others, to analyze needs, to retrieve data, to instruct users, to manage operations and supervise staff who provide services—are the same whether or not automated resources are used.

Three papers consider the competencies required by professionals working in different types of libraries. Reflecting on "The Public Librarian of the Last Years of the Twentieth Century," Richard T. Sweeney enumerates six new competency areas for public librarians: (1) managing information technology; (2) keeping informed about the state-of-the-art of specific information technologies; (3) monitoring future or developing information technologies; (4) analyzing information-seeking behavior; (5) understanding the societal issues that develop from the information technology; and (6) building knowledge bases. In her paper on "Technology and the Academic Library Staff or the Resurgence of the Luddites," Carolyn M. Gray emphasizes the importance of people in the successful planning and implementation of library automation. Pointing out the kinship of special librarians with the one-man band, Hillis L. Griffin illustrates some of the unique challenges in the one-person library as "Special Librarians Face the New Technology."

In-service training, graduate professional education and professional societies can all contribute to the development of competencies. Linda Baskin and Mima Spencer provide specific guidelines for "Training Staff to Use Computers." Drawing from their experience as trainers, they share their insights on how learning about computers differs from and is similar to other training. In "Education Matters," Evelyn H. Daniel describes three models for change in library/information educational programs: incremental, conceptual/futurist, and skill-oriented. She illustrates the advantages and disadvantages of the competency-based approach for education by describing the process by which the School Media Specialist/ Computer Task Force at Syracuse University identified competencies for the building-level computer coordinator in schools. In her paper on "The Role of the Association in Developing Professional Competence," Julie Carroll Virgo discusses multiple roles: highlighting "good" or innovative practice, setting educational standards, providing an environment where leadership and group skills can be developed, providing opportunities to learn new technical skills or knowledge and to exchange ideas, disseminating information, and providing continuing education programs. She also introduces a number of challenges and constraints facing associations and suggests directions for future association efforts.

Recognizing the growing involvement of libraries of all types in networking and cooperative activities, Jo An S. Segal concludes the papers in this volume with a discussion of "Competencies for Library Networking and Cooperation." In her view, competencies for librarians working in cooperative agencies fall in seven categories: communication theory and practice, teaching and training competencies, mastery of the field of librarianship, knowledge of specific systems which form the basis for the service of the agency, business administration, planning ability and skills, and clarification of values. She also identifies competencies necessary for librarians in order to make them effective users of networks and of library technology.

Although the speakers at the Clinic were drawn from organizations in the United States, the topic of professional competencies in relation to technology is of concern wherever new information technologies are being applied to library and information work.[1] Similarly, the topic should be of interest to information professionals with varying responsibilities: faculty of graduate professional programs, others involved in training and education, administrators concerned with staff development, and individuals seeking to fill positions which make use of technology. Earlier volumes in this series of Clinic proceedings have documented the many ways in which computers and other information technologies are being used in libraries and related information services. It is hoped that the present volume, with its focus on the human factor, will encourage consideration of how best to develop our human resources to make effective use of technology for human ends.

LINDA C. SMITH
Editor

REFERENCE

1. See, for example: Wight, Tony. *A Discourse on Issues: An Exploratory Study of the Implications of Information Technology for U.K. Library & Information Work Manpower Planning* (British Library Research and Development Report No. 5656). London: Aslib Research & Consultancy Division, 1980.

JOSÉ-MARIE GRIFFITHS
Vice President
King Research, Inc.

Competency Requirements for Library and Information Science Professionals

One of the paradoxes of the phenomenal growth of the information community is that librarianship, one of the oldest and most respected of information professions, is experiencing great difficulties as a profession at a time when it should be experiencing its greatest growth. There are many hypotheses as to why this is happening. One is that the environment and new technologies are changing the patterns of distribution of the work force and the ways in which information is being communicated. There are many who feel that librarians as intermediaries will cease to exist. It is my contention that these changes will increase the importance of librarians, albeit in possible new roles in addition to their existing ones. Another hypothesis is that the changing environment and new technologies are not being fully met by educational institutions. A likely reason for these needs and demands not being fully met is a lack of communication between the employers of information professionals and the institutions that educate and train them.

The survey of information professionals conducted by the University of Pittsburgh and King Research, Inc. and the work conducted to date on the project "New Directions in Library and Information Science Education" suggest that this lack of communication occurs because needed competencies are not well described, and library and information science schools and other education and training organizations are not communicating well with those who employ information professionals. The channels for communication of information concerning the changing demand for specific competencies are displayed in figure 1.

There are several basic levels of communication which can clarify the changing requirements of the information science profession and aid in

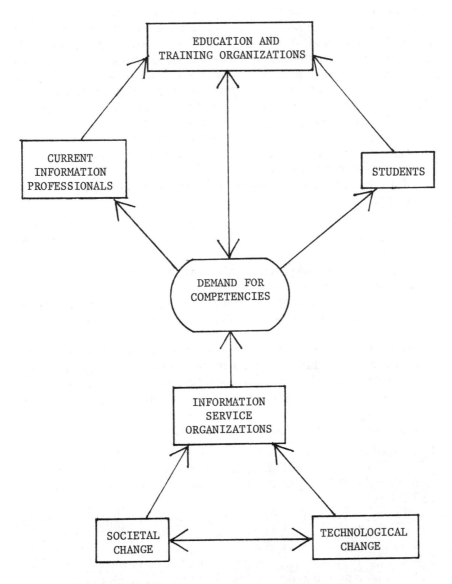

Fig. 1. Current Communication Channels for Information
Concerning Demand for Competencies

determining the most appropriate response for the education and training organizations. The entire communications process can be viewed as being driven by technological, societal and other environmental changes. As these changes are continuous (sometimes fast, sometimes slow) so should the communications process be continuous and responsive. Unfortunately, this is rarely the case. The problem addressed by the remainder of this paper is how can the education and training of information professionals be made appropriate to the rapidly changing information environment so that professionals can perform their jobs effectively. In a rapidly changing environment the effects of the communications gap referred to above will become more severe.

In order to address this problem the following questions need to be considered:

1. What are the current major trends affecting the library and information environment? To what extent will the environment change in the future?
2. What do information professionals do? What functions and activities do they perform? Where do they work?
3. What aspects of the functions and activities performed by information professionals will change given the trends described above in question 1?
4. What competencies are currently needed by information professionals to perform their functions and activities? What new competencies will be needed? Which competencies will become more prominent?
5. To what extent do information professionals currently possess the necessary competencies identified above in question 4?
6. How can future competency needs be met?

In beginning to answer some of these questions, the U.S. Department of Education contracted with King Research, Inc. to identify current and future competency requirements of librarians and other information professionals.

The approach to the project taken by King Research is not to attempt an extensive forecast into future needs, but rather to initiate a process that will support the future planning of education and training programs for information professionals. The process will be concerned with both formal education as well as continuing education so that information professionals will be able to acquire appropriate and necessary competencies in a timely fashion as the external information environment changes.

The project framework (as it has been developed to date) describes trends which affect library and information science organizations, the work settings in which library and information professionals perform, and the functions and activities performed. Also considered are the types of users served, the tools and techniques used/applied, and the types of materials handled. Each of these dimensions serves to distinguish various sets of competencies.

Competencies are defined as comprising one or more of the following components:

Knowledge
—of librarianship and information science
—of specific subject areas (e.g., chemistry, law)

Skills
—cognitive
—analytical
—technical
—interpersonal
—basic literacy/numeracy

Attitudes
—toward the profession
—motivational

Some of the major trends identified through the literature and through interactions with information professionals are:

—increases in availability of automated tools for storing, processing and retrieving information;
—increases in the volume and types of materials available;
—increases in networking and resource-sharing activities;
—increases in the demand for information services; and
—increases in the awareness and sophistication of information users.

This list is by no means exhaustive but represents some of the major trends that affect information professional competency requirements. The exact nature of this relationship has yet to be determined.

In defining work settings an attempt was made to represent a range of settings within which information professionals will be found in the foreseeable future. A preliminary list of work settings includes:

—libraries;
—information centers and clearinghouses;
—database producers;
—database distributors and services;
—special collections (e.g., museums) and archives;
—information analysis centers;
—information service companies (e.g., brokers, jobbers, consultants);
—project support groups; and
—records systems or centers.

Broad functions performed by the library and information professionals have been defined across work settings. They are grouped under three general headings: user-oriented, technical and support. Conceptually, these subgroupings reflect the degree to which the activities performed within that function involve users. Thus, user-oriented functions involve direct interactions with users or activities performed in direct response to user requests. Technical functions involve the collection management aspects of a library or an information service which affect end-users only indirectly. Support functions include those additional functions which are necessary to perform user-oriented and technical functions but which may have little direct effect on end-users. For this project the importance of the functional groupings selected is their correspondence with types of competencies required. Within the functional groupings, further breakdowns have been established as listed below. An attempt was made to make the terminology of functions as generic as possible across the range of functions performed in a variety of work settings.

User-Oriented Functions
  Needs Analysis
  Searching
  Retrieval
  Analysis of Information
  Dissemination
  User Training
  Program Presentation

Technical Functions
  Creation and Recording
  Production
  Collection Development
  Description and Organization
  Storage and Maintenance
  Disposal/Weeding
  Recordkeeping

Support Functions
  Administration
    Management
    Planning
    Accounting and Finance
    Policies and Procedures
    Personnel and Staff Development
    Facilities Management
    Communications

Marketing
    Systems Analysis and Design
    Research and Development

The development of this framework has helped to identify many different aspects of the information profession today, especially in defining its boundaries. In planning education and training programs for information professionals we have defined a total process, part of which has been described in some detail earlier. The overall planning process is shown in figure 2.

The planning framework establishes an ongoing and timely feedback among information service organizations (ISOs), education and training organizations (ETOs), professional societies, the relevant information research community, and individuals within them. The first step in the planning cycle is to describe the universe of participating organizations (i.e., ISOs, ETOs, professional societies, and research organizations). The second step is to determine the population of library and information professionals who are or who would be affected by new education and training curricula. Parallel to this step is the need to describe education and training activities as well as faculty and students involved in ETOs and professional societies. Also at this stage it is useful to describe current and planned research and development activities relating to competencies and to establish the stimuli that might affect the competency requirements, such as new technology and societal change. The next step involves activities necessary to determine required competencies. These activities include: (1) defining the ISO mission, information-related jobs, and skills necessary to perform these jobs; (2) determining current (and planned) competencies that are taught by ETOs and professional societies; and (3) assessing completed and current research and development in the areas of competencies, library and information science, technology, and societal changes. At that point, the required competencies will be identified, defined, described, and validated (the scope of the ongoing project).

The next step in the overall planning process will be to determine education and training requirements necessary to support the attainment of these competencies. After that is done, it will be necessary to design curricula and implement them in test sites. In parallel, competency attainment measures based on education and training requirements and knowledge of what has been found in competency research should be defined and implemented. The implemented curricula can then be evaluated in terms of the competency attainment measures. Such evaluation might lead to new and/or revised education and training requirements. Since much of the curricula evaluation will be in ISO sites, the results may also yield better definitions and determination of library and information profes-

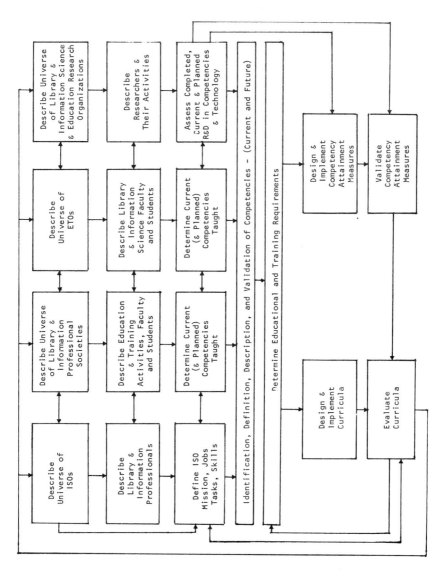

Fig. 2. A Planning Framework for Determining New Directions
in Library and Information Science Education

sional jobs, tasks and skills. Finally, the evaluation should lead to updated descriptions of the universe of participants. The entire cycle is regenerative and should establish new competencies to reflect changes in the dynamic information environment. The overall process should allow for the most appropriate and timely formal and continuing education for information professionals rendering them more competent and, therefore, effective performers.

KATHRYN LUTHER HENDERSON
Associate Professor
Graduate School of Library and Information Science
University of Illinois at Urbana-Champaign

The New Technology and Competencies for "The Most Typical of the Activities of Libraries": Technical Services

INTRODUCTION

At a library conference in 1940, William M. Randall called technical services the "most typical of the activities of libraries"—"they are..." he said, "the things which librarians do that no one else does—the secrets of the craft."[1] In those intervening forty-three years much has been written and uttered in defense and derision of these "secrets of the craft." These most typical of library activities have changed the name Randall used, technical *processes*, to technical *services*. They have moved from being sneeringly derided as "backroom," "basement" or other dreary location activities to being enthusiastically hailed today as "where the action is." They are, fortunately, no longer the "secrets" that they were in Randall's day. They have been moved into, moved around within and even moved out of the organizational charts. Regardless of all these attitudes and activities, the functions of acquiring, organizing and preserving library materials persist and the competencies necessary to carry out these three functions will be the focus of this paper. In the paper, reference will frequently be made to the "technical services librarian" meaning any librarian who works in that aspect of librarianship. The emphasis is on no particular type of library. The term *library* will be used as meaning also information center.

Several means, in addition to relying upon experience, observation and a perusal of the literature, were used to gain insights into how the profession views contemporary and future competencies for technical services. First of all, the technical services competencies called for in job announcement listings found in *The Chronicle of Higher Education*[2] and the *LJ/SLJ Hotline*[3] for September-December 1982 were studied. To obtain a better representation of data from other than university libraries, eighteen job announcements for positions in settings other than university libraries were obtained from the Placement Office, Graduate School of Library and Information Science (GSLIS), University of Illinois at Urbana-Champaign (UIUC). A total of 188 job announcements were identified and coded according to several categories.[4] Librarians who are either now or have recently been actively engaged in technical services related work were surveyed to ascertain their ideas. The librarians were chosen from GSLIS, UIUC graduates. This method of selection does not satisfy the rigors of scientific sampling; nevertheless, the forty-three persons responding to the survey had a wide range of responsibilities covering all aspects of the technical services including administration as well as representing the vendor, network and foundation communities.[5] In some cases the respondents sought opinions of other staff members thereby adding to the original number of respondents. Professional experience varied from a few months in the field to nineteen years and covered all types of libraries located from New York to California and from Minnesota to Texas. Their replies were filled with many insights and ideas. Although some of them had entered the field before the new technologies had really taken hold, these librarians have proved their ability to plan for, implement and manage work related to the new technologies.

An analysis of all the data revealed that the competencies fall into essentially two main groupings which will form the outline for this paper: (1) general, technical and bibliographic competencies; and (2) managerial, supervisory, organizational and communications competencies. In reality, however, categorization does not fall neatly into these areas—there will tend to be some overlap—e.g., technical competencies are interspersed throughout the discussion. Some of these competencies are not exclusive to technical services but are especially pertinent to that area of work at this point in time and that is the reason for their inclusion here.

GENERAL, TECHNICAL AND BIBLIOGRAPHIC COMPETENCIES

General Competencies

From the analysis of the 188 job announcements, 65.4 percent were for positions in university libraries; 18.1 percent for public; 9 percent for colleges; 3.2 percent for community colleges; 2.7 percent for special libraries; and 1.6 percent for other types (see table 1).

TABLE 1
TYPES OF LIBRARIES LISTING
TECHNICAL SERVICES POSITIONS

	n=188	
	Number	Percentage
University	123	65.4
Public	34	18.1
College	17	9.0
Community college	6	3.2
Special	5	2.7
Other	3	1.6
Total	188	100.0

Of the 182 positions which fall within definable categories, 61.6 percent were cataloging positions (9 positions were specifically for serials catalogers). Positions described no more specifically than technical services positions accounted for 21.4 percent while 4.9 percent of the positions were advertised as acquisitions positions (two-thirds of them were serials acquisitions positions). Another 4.9 percent were advertised as automation positions that included some aspects of the technical services as well (e.g., automation and retrospective conversion librarian; assistant catalog librarian and automation specialist; assistant director for automated systems and technical services; and an adult public services librarian in a public library who was also to carry responsibilities for technical services including conversion of data to an online catalog and development of an online circulation system—the latter position representing a truly wholistic librarian!). From the analysis of the positions, 4.4 percent were as administrators in more than one specific unit (but not all units) of the technical services while 1.7 percent asked for persons to work in technical services in children's sections and 1.1 percent were for general serials positions (see table 2).

Although more of an educational requirement than a competency, the master's degree in library and information science is still considered a necessity as 68.7 percent of the 188 positions in the study called for the degree from an institution accredited by the American Library Association (ALA) while 22.3 percent required the degree without specifying that it come from an ALA accredited institution. Therefore, a total of 91 percent of the 188 positions listed in the sources noted above called for a master's degree in library and information science (see table 3). Backgrounds in specialized areas varying from Oriental art (at the graduate level) to music and from biochemistry to law were specified in 32.9 percent (62) of the

TABLE 2
TECHNICAL SERVICES POSITIONS
(DEFINABLE CATEGORIES BY CATEGORIES DESCRIBED)

| | *n=182* | |
	Number	*Percentage*
Cataloging		
(includes 9 serials cataloging positions)	112	61.6
Technical services	39	21.4
Acquisitions		
(includes 6 serials acquisitions positions)	9	4.9
Automation		
(including some technical services responsibilities)	9	4.9
Administration of several (but not all)		
technical services units	8	4.4
Technical services work in children's sections	3	1.7
General serials	2	1.1
Total	182	100.0

TABLE 3
SPECIFIED MASTER'S DEGREE IN
LIBRARY/INFORMATION SCIENCE

| | *n=188* | |
	Number	*Percentage*
From ALA accredited schools	129	68.7
ALA accreditation not specified	42	22.3
Not specified	17	9.0
Total	188	100.0

positions while 9.6 percent (18) required or found desirable a second master's degree or some other advanced degree in a special subject. Two positions required Medical Library Association certification.

Traditional competencies in foreign languages are holding their own by being requested in 42.6 percent (80) of the 188 positions. Of these eighty requests, 61.3 percent were couched in general terms such as "Western European"; "European"; "two" or "Romance" languages; or simply "a language is helpful"; but 38.7 percent (31) specified particular language requirements (see table 4) with 29 percent of the 31 calling for German; 16.1 percent for French; 12.9 percent each for Spanish and Russian; 9.7 percent for Arabic and/or Hebrew; 6.5 percent for Latin and/or Greek; 6.5 percent for Italian; and 3.2 percent each for Chinese and for a Slavic language (see table 5). Foreign languages were also believed to be important in a number of the survey replies for reasons well summarized by Richard A. Stewart: "we desperately need to start widening foreign-language competence among librarians as the information network continues to become more international and as our own country continues to enrich its culture with immigrants."[6] It should be noted that this need for language competencies was not just expressed by those employed in university and college libraries but by those who worked in other types of libraries as well. (Stewart himself is a cataloger in a public library.)

TABLE 4
LANGUAGES SPECIFIED

	n=80	
	Number	Percentage
General terms (e.g., "two," "romance")	49	61.3
Specific languages designated	31	38.7
Total	80	100.0

TABLE 5
SPECIFIC LANGUAGES DESIGNATED

	n=31	
	Number	Percentage
German	9	29.0
French	5	16.1
Spanish	4	12.9
Russian	4	12.9
Arabic/Hebrew	3	9.7
Latin/Greek	2	6.5
Italian	2	6.5
Chinese	1	3.2
Slavic	1	3.2
Total	31	100.0

In the position listings, technological competencies were mentioned in two different ways: those calling for "knowledge of" a particular or general category of technology and those calling for "experience with" technology. "Knowledge of" competencies were described ten times in terms implying knowledge of "computer applications and technology" while other terms used less frequently called for knowledge of integrated library systems, automated serials and cataloging, systems analysis, data processing to support acquisitions and book fund accounting, keyboarding skills, and retrospective conversion. Some "technological" experience (most frequently with OCLC) was requested in 25 percent of the listings. However, traditional experience, particularly cataloging, outdistanced technological experience by being called for in 50 percent of the job listings.

In the survey sent to technical services librarians many specific and general technological skills were mentioned. Keith Russell's statement serves as a concise summary statement calling for:

> the ability to understand the technology (in a general way); interest in the technology; ability to understand (and change) workflow; ability to find out what one needs to know about the technology; knowledge of whom to trust and believe; ability to work effectively with systems people and vendors (and to treat promises with appropriate reservation and skepticism); and vision to see beyond the department and the library....[7]

Lacking in the job announcements but mentioned frequently in the survey replies was the commitment to *service* for the library user—the very reason for the existence of the technical services (or public services for that matter)! In order to give dedicated services to library users, the librarian must be competent in defining goals and objectives. Once again Randall's words of over four decades ago speak to technical services workers today: "The knowledge we need to define the objectives of a given library or class of libraries is a knowledge of the needs of library users; a knowledge of their abilities to employ the resources peculiar to libraries to satisfy their needs and a knowledge of the resources themselves."[8]

Bibliographic Competencies

The importance of bibliographic competencies permeated the survey answers. How can one work in library services of any type today without them? Bibliographic competencies are the very skills of librarianship itself—they are necessary to acquire, organize and preserve library materials—and technology changes them. These competencies will be considered under several different categories.

The Materials Acquired and the Sources for Acquiring Them

Librarians have always needed to know what materials should be acquired and the sources for acquiring them. But technology is affecting both the materials and the sources. Only a few of the ways this is happening can be mentioned here.

Major electronic, computer and other media companies now control many publishing firms resulting, in some cases, in a change in the quality of materials as well as in the relationships with old, long established, family businesses. Dealing with the new houses and selecting from their publications requires new skills as does recognition of changes brought about by those aspects of electronic publishing that use computers to facilitate the production of printed products. In the future, shorter print runs should be more economical through the introduction of computerized composition and production.[9] As publishers are eventually able to place such systems in-house, they should be able to make available books on current topics more quickly.

However, Judy McDermott warns that there is a good news/bad news syndrome at work here: acquisitions librarians may not be able to find out about the publications before they are temporarily out-of-stock or out-of-print.[10] While additional start-up costs for a second print run will be lower as the text is already online, publishers will still have to see a demand for a title before investing in additional runs. Publishing on demand may be a real possibility in the future but may not be so until publishers can afford, and markets are viable, to foster such programs. Print media reviews will be too slow to inform librarians of these short runs therefore items may be temporarily or permanently unavailable by the time the orders are placed. Acquisitions personnel will find the need to develop new competencies in locating information about publications because even the distributors of prepublication bibliographic information will have less time to disseminate the bibliographic information to which we have become accustomed. McDermott suggests that acquisitions librarians will need to "approach acquisitions work more aggressively."[11]

Thomas Hickey predicts that in the not too distant future a large proportion of the current journal literature will be available online.[12] This will require "subscriptions" that are totally new to acquisitions and serials librarians. Evidence that online subscriptions are beginning to appear comes from the announcement that on 1 June 1983, the full text of all the primary journals of the American Chemical Society will be available online through Bibliographic Retrieval Services, Inc. (BRS) which already offers the full text of the *Harvard Business Review* online and is prepared to offer online service for the medical journals of the Elsevier Science Publishing Company in the future.[13] Other publishers are exploring the issuing of journals on videodiscs and making copies available for a fee.[14] New competencies will be required to obtain, organize and maintain materials through these newer dissemination methods.

The recent introduction of microcomputers into educational settings requires competencies in the selection of software which can frequently best be obtained from personal visits to local vendors.[15] To learn about the selection of software packages, the acquisitions librarian may be found reading from selection materials outside his/her usual realm. In addition to knowing about the software, acquisitions personnel must become knowledgeable about the documentation that accompanies the software taking into account what seems suitable to the needs and expertise of the intended users. It follows that the librarian will need to be knowledgeable enough about the hardware to be sure that the software is compatible with the equipment to operate it. The acquisitions librarian should also be aware that any program can have a "bug" in it and should be prepared to deal with the return of the package.

There are other library problems associated with software than those related to acquisitions. First of all, the *Anglo-American Cataloguing Rules,* second edition (AACR2)[16] were formulated prior to the introduction of microcomputers; and the specific rules in AACR2's chapter 9 ("Machine-Readable Data Files")[17] are not readily adaptable for this type of material. School librarians, in particular, are voicing difficulties with processing this type of material. For the time being, librarians will find Sue A. Dodd's *Cataloging Machine-Readable Data Files*[18] a helpful tool to use in deciding how to handle this type of material. Secondly, new preservation problems are posed by software in libraries. The susceptibility of the software to damage from lightning, storms and high winds which cause power outages as well as from static electricity cannot be overlooked by the preservation librarian.[19] Users too must be educated about damage that can come to software. Emard has prepared a list of "do nots" that could well become a part of the instructions given to users of microcomputer disks in order to protect this new carrier of information.[20]

Microcomputers offer much in the way of word processing capabilities to take care of many of the correspondence details associated with the acquisitions process; therefore, paraprofessionals should be better able to handle an increasing amount of this work. Maximizing these and other capabilities of microcomputers such as employing software packages for budgeting, forecasting and planning will become an important area of supervisory expertise for the acquisitions staff.

With the noted coming changes in publishing, new and speedier means are required to obtain the publications. Librarians, publishers and vendors will seek new means to order materials; therefore the librarian must become competent in evaluating the differing capabilities and costs of each system to meet the needs of the local institution and to recognize that capabilities and costs vary from vendor to vendor—and are constantly changing—and all the while, the field to choose from grows larger and the choices more difficult.[21]

The Tools that are Used

The tools used in technical services operations that come from outside the library have for some time, in one way or another, been affected by the new technologies; in turn, they affect work strategies in the local library. Many of the tools used in the past for verification of orders are no longer used in the same way, if used at all. Until the new shorter runs spoken about earlier become commonplace, the first, and often the only, tool needed for verification is the database of a bibliographic utility.[22] This is especially so as the databases have come to include cataloging-in-publication data. For items not yet in the database, new routines must be established for re-searching the databases taking into account published studies that can help determine the optimum time lapse between searches.[23]

Using these databases for any technical services function requires competency in the appropriate search strategies for each situation to save valuable time for the library staff as well as to decrease time spent on the system thereby helping to assure better response time and reduced costs for all users of the system.[24] Search strategies will become important in other ways; for example, some old familiar verification tools such as Bowker's *Books in Print* (BIP)[25] and *Ulrich's International Periodicals Directory*[26] are now online, but they are not identical, mirror images of their paper siblings.[27] The acquisitions personnel must know when to use the hard copies and when it is economical to use the enhanced search capabilities of their online counterparts each possibly with different search commands from other online systems.

The Tools that are Made: The Role of Bibliographic and Technical Standards

The hallmark of the technical services has been its record keeping tasks to support a variety of paper files. Each of these files, in its separate location, covered records necessary for processes from acquisitions through binding. Frequently, in the past, these files have demonstrated little consistency in format or content in relation to other files. When the same integrated file is shared by all local users within any one library and as more of the files are shared among libraries through online cooperative services, the need for consistency through bibliographic standards has increased. While at one time the new technologies were expected—because of their new search capabilities—to abrogate the need for such standards, quite the opposite effect has actually occurred at least in the past decade. Now, a larger proportion of the time and talent of the technical services librarian is occupied with standards (and learning the acronyms that name them!).

Cataloging codes are among our oldest standards and have for over 125 years been acknowledged as a necessity for cooperative efforts. Their continued importance was acknowledged by virtually all persons answering the survey. Knowledge of the present code as well as previous codes is essential (e.g., in retrospective conversion activities and in understanding and interpreting the catalog). However, in the job announcements only 7 percent (14) of the jobs advertised called for knowledge of the *Anglo-American Cataloging Rules,* first edition (AACR1)[28] while 31 percent (59) requested knowledge of AACR2. Perhaps a knowledge is presumed but this is not the best way to write a job announcement if such knowledge is expected.

While at one time catalogers were the librarians primarily concerned with standards, this is no longer the case. An acquisitions librarian entering an item which does not appear in the OCLC (Online Computer Library Center) Online Union Catalog into the OCLC Acquisition Subsystem is expected to format the record according to the standards of AACR2.[29] Every librarian in a local system finds it necessary to interpret not only local records but also those found in MARC[30] (or other machine readable) formats of the online bibliographic services, yet only 10 percent (20) of the 188 job announcements requested knowledge of MARC formats while knowledge of the OCLC system (and possibly its formats) was called for in 25.6 percent (48) of the listings. Serial librarians engaged in union listing efforts are likely to be describing serials holdings according to the summary level standards set by the American National Standards Institute (ANSI Z39.42) which have been adopted as the approved medium by the OCLC Serial Union Listing Capability.[31]

While the MARC format identifies and tags the data elements for the electronic transmission of bibliographic data, MARC does not specify the bibliographic content of the record; therefore, standards in the form of the National Level Bibliographic Record (NLBR)[32] are devised so that an organization creating records in machine-readable form for its use will also be creating acceptable records content-wise for sharing with other organizations or for contributing to a national database.

As a large supply of bibliographic data emanates from the Library of Congress (LC), that library serves as a role model for cataloging standards. LC's policies have a strong influence on those of other libraries as well as the bibliographic utilities. Knowledge of the Library of Congress Rule Interpretations (LCRIs)[33] for AACR2 and their frequent changes are almost as essential as knowledge of AACR2 itself, especially when the bibliographic utility mandates their application.

The attempts at cooperation brought about by the new technologies have found the technical services librarian rediscovering an old, almost forgotten, competency—the building of authority control mechanisms now, not only for the local library, but for other libraries as well through cooperative programs such as the Name Authority Cooperative (NACO) Project sponsored by the Library of Congress.[34] Later this year the Washington Library Network, the Research Libraries Group, and the Library of Congress will choose the sharing of authority records as the first application of the Linked Systems Project.[35] This online communications link and intersystem data retrieval and maintenance facility "will enable heterogeneous computer systems to exchange data, and is extensible to additional systems beyond the initial three," according to Wayne E. Davison and is based on existing and emerging international standards as much as is possible.[36] The resurging necessity for authority control brings forth a National Level Authority Record to help set the standard for data elements that should be included by an organization creating authority records in machine-readable form for sharing with other institutions or contributing to a nationwide database.[37]

The new technologies call for a variety of technical standards and these too must become a part of the knowledge base for the technical services librarian. Hickey and Spies tell us that:

> Without some standardization, the marketplace becomes fragmented. Information services and products will not break through on any large scale unless the user is assured of easy, trouble-free use. It is, therefore, important to standardize various aspects of the presentation format component of library and information systems to the extent to which they will meet the requirements of the majority of potential users.[38]

Technical services are affected by standards from other parts of the information community such as those developed by the Books Industry Systems Advisory Committee (BISAC) for a standard purchase order communications format to facilitate computer-to-computer ordering. This standard will be incorporated into the design of online acquisitions systems of OCLC, the Washington Library Network, CLSI, and Dataphase. Locally developed in-house automated systems are encouraged to use this format too.[39]

More and more, our standards become international in nature looking ahead to increased sharing of data as is evident by the use of the International Standard Book Number (ISBN) as the primary identifier in the BISAC order format;[40] the incorporation of the International Standard Bibliographical Description (ISBD) formats into AACR2 and the use of the International Standard Serial Number (ISSN) in a variety of ways. Developed as a national standard, MARC also goes international with UNIMARC. Specifications have been prepared to convert the U.S. MARC format into the UNIMARC format and it is expected that the Library of Congress will have the capability to distribute MARC cataloging data in the UNIMARC format in the near future.[41]

Standards must be revised and changed and that in turn changes other standards. Changes in cataloging codes brought about changes in MARC and OCLC formats. There are defects in the ISBN system so committees are at work to develop a machine generated Universal Standard Book Code to replace it.[42] And if no one standard is settled upon, then, competing means arise such as is presently occurring in the identification of microcomputer software where at least three different coding systems are being developed to serve purposes similar to ISBN: the Universal Software Market Identifier (USMI) being developed by Technique Learning Corporation in conjunction with the Association of Data Processing Service Organizations; the International Standard Program Number (ISPN) created by Imprint Software Incorporated; and a five digit number which classifies the software into one of sixty-five categories as well as by title being produced by Visual Materials Incorporated along with WIDL Video. At the same time R.R. Bowker contends that as the agency responsible for ISBN numbering, Bowker is thereby authorized to assign ISBN numbers to computer software.[43] Until one of these systems or yet another system becomes the accepted standard, technical services personnel will find it necessary to be acquainted with each system.

Still new standards continue to be promulgated or considered. An ANSI Subcommittee, Z39, Subcommittee G (Standard Terms, Abbreviations and Symbols for Use in Interactive Information Retrieval) is searching for guidelines as to whether a standard online common command language is desirable for gaining access to a variety of databases instead of the required mastering of a number of different languages.[44]

Tools That We Make: The Online Format
Except for a brief fling with the book catalog in mid-century, librarians have found the physical format of the twentieth-century tools that they have made to vary little. A stable and settled format such as the card format has enjoyed calls for few decisions in that regard. One accepts what the technology allows. Now technology allows viable alternatives—COM online and who knows what else even today is being invented in the dorm of some Stanford undergrad or in Silicon Valley. And now the librarian must decide not only the best format to use to meet the needs of the local clientele, but, if the choice involves the new technologies, decisions must be made between vendor-produced systems, in-house developments or borrowing from previously developed systems that offer the chosen format.

Paper files existed independently from other files. Now the opportunity for interfacing is near—a totally integrated local system cannot be far off. A whole new tool for librarian and library user alike is about to be born. A different approach must be taken by designer and user for this new tool. There are few examples to chart the course—there are few who have passed this way before. This is the time to take into account the reminder of Shoshana Zuboff that information technology, by creating a medium where imagination instead of experience-based judgment is important, challenges our old procedures, and according to Zuboff: "Judging a task in light of experience thus becomes less important than imagining how the task can be reorganized based on new technical capabilities."[45] So imagination and creativity must be among the attributes of technical services librarians who build the new tools to meet the needs of local users, many of whom have become computer literate themselves. The computer literate user knows the capabilities of computers and will expect much more from the new tools than he/she did from the old.

Being creative and imaginative in making the new tool does not preclude understanding how to build a total catalog—one with integrity— even though the new tool will certainly relate and collocate in quite a different way from the old. Sara Stephan, one of the respondents to the survey of technical services librarians, indicates that being concerned about making a total catalog is somewhat easier with the card catalog because the physical entity is there to remind you of the necessity, and "when working online it is easy to forget about the other thousands of records in the system and see only the one that you are working with."[46] She notes that with changes in cataloging rules, filing systems and others tools, the necessity still remains to remember how changes must also take place in authority records and in the tagging of the fields to be retreived. Frederick Kilgour too has pointed out that, in online systems, librarians are often too concerned about making an individual bibliographic record rather than "constructing a catalog."[47] Meanwhile, Nancy F. Carter cautions that, "the sound philosophy of cataloging should not be deleted in favor of mechanics and 'new toys.' "[48] These are but a few reminders that making an automated catalog is not an automatic process—it still requires knowing what a catalog is intended to do in addition to lots of work and thought to achieve the goals that are set for it.

Being imaginative and creative does not preclude learning all that is possible from the studies of existing online catalogs and research into the requirements of future catalogs conducted by the Council on Library Resources, OCLC and other institutions and from the wise counsel of Charles Hildreth,[49] Stephen Salmon,[50] Joseph Matthews,[51] and MELVYL team,[52] and others. But reading these studies should quickly tell us that careful and often lengthy planning is necessary to make a truly "user friendly" tool. The studies give us some pause to reconsider long held beliefs such as those which have claimed that known-items searches are of much more importance to the user than are subject searches. That is not the message from the new studies[53] and our century-long dedication to perfecting descriptive cataloging must now find equal dedication to perfecting subject access—in a much shorter time frame. A really imaginative person can even devise ways to use classification as a tool for organization of subject content within the catalog rather than its long established predominant use as a shelf location device—and existing schemes may not be the ones to provide for the new use.

Content is not the only concern in making the new tools. Some knowledge of the internal organization of files will be helpful. Command languages will need to be devised that are user friendly and terminals will need to be chosen that are as easy to use as possible while still being responsive to the multiple and diverse needs of users. Of great help to the librarian should be the record-keeping capabilities of the computer and the creation of statistics. Meaningful interpretation and use of the statistics should help in continual design and redesign of a responsive tool. Therefore research on the local level and sharing the results of that research through publication will be an important part of the librarian's work. These findings and new developments will result in dynamic, ever changing tools, for the new technologies never stand still. Even now, as we are immersed in national and international standards and in the creation of networks and other cooperative efforts, the advances in hardware and the services offered by the increasing number of commercial vendors are making the possibility of creating local systems responsive to the needs of local users much more of a reality. Richard DeGennaro has written about the multiple options of the 1980s, speaking of the increasing possibility "for a library to put together multifunction library systems from the functional components of several different vendors with appropriate links as interfaces. Thus, as the various subsystem components become obsolete, they can be replaced with the latest and best components on the market."[54] Add open-mindedness to the competencies list for the 1980s.

The Materials Preserved: Conservation/Preservation Competencies[55]

Record keeping for the activities of preserving library materials has, for a long time, been more than a local activity. Long since paper rubbings were made to send to the binder for assuring consistency in physical format for volumes of the same serial or series. Later, sample backs, or full-sized examples on buckram strips of the stamping patterns for titles bound for a customer came into use to create standardized prescriptions for commonly held titles. These methods, however, often proved restrictive for individual libraries and by the 1960s binders were making use of embossed plates to carry the standardized information. In the mid-1970s the content of the embossed plates was converted to machine-readable form to develop computer-assisted systems for storing and reproducing that part of the binding record which was relatively constant. By the end of that decade, the advent of minicomputers and computer driven stamping equipment brought dreams of interactive systems, linking binderies and libraries much closer. In the 1980s, these dreams are just now becoming realities as some binding departments are just now beginning to experience some freedom from many paper files and from the copying of records many times over.

Binderies use computers in a variety of ways in the binding process although much of the process still is human-intensive. New competencies must be developed to ascertain the effect of these new operations on the materials as well as to write specifications for new contracts.

Knowledge of developments in both computer applications and preservation filming is a necessity in preservation work today. In the future, the videodisc holds promise of becoming a new storage medium if costs can be reduced and other problems resolved.[56] One disk is reported to have the capability of storing 54,000 frames per side which means storing 54,000 photographs or 13,500 pages of text per side.[57] The Library of Congress is engaged in several pilot projects using laser optical disk technology for information and preservation management.[58] While general use is not anticipated for some time, the technical services librarian must include knowing about and following the progress of this new technology among his/her competencies.

Establishing environmental conditions for materials involves the preservation librarian and many others with heating, cooling, humidifying, dehumidifying, air filtering, and scrubbing techniques. Many of these techniques are computer-controlled locally and the preservation librarian needs to develop a competency in monitoring these activities (at times aggressively) and their effect on the local collection. Chemical technology, too, has become an important component in developing improved paper, adhesives and preservation supplies as well as deacidification techniques.

As online databases develop, the preservation librarian should insist that preservation copies be identified on the records. Such information is helpful not only to local users but aids network members as well. Since its inception, the Research Libraries Group (RLG) has supported the idea of indicating conservation/preservation efforts through the RLIN system (Research Libraries Information Network) where indication of the quality of materials and the location of master microforms would be noted. Enhancements to the system are expected soon.[59] SOLINET (Southeastern Library Network) is also considering such efforts according to Frank P. Grisham.[60]

MANAGERIAL, SUPERVISORY AND COMMUNICATIVE COMPETENCIES

Increasingly, librarians who work in the technical services area are called upon to be managers, supervisors and communicators. They have always assumed these roles, of course, but certain aspects of the roles are of greater importance because of the introduction of the new technologies.

Of prime importance is the identification of problems and working toward the solutions of these problems. Whether the librarian is the head of the department, an original cataloger, an acquisitions or preservation librarian, or a serials manager, problems that need to be solved are encountered. Some problems can be easily identified and even solved. Others are of greater magnitude. All require problem solvers, planners and decision makers at various levels in the organization. Solving a problem after it has been identified consists of several important steps that are likely to take considerable time, effort and expertise when the new technologies are involved. Therefore it is not likely (or advisable) that the problems of larger magnitude (or even some of the smaller ones) can be solved in isolation. Technical services operations usually affect the total library system; therefore several opinions need to be heard in the planning phase. Then, too, no one person can identify all the needs, read and comprehend all the literature, make all the on-site visits, determine all the hardware and software requirements, and all the other aspects involved in planning for the new technologies.

Richard Boss identifies the steps that are to be taken in this process as: first of all, defining the problem, spelling out the purpose of the project, setting its scope, and determining the budget available.[61] This may require seeking expert advice outside the library staff by bringing in a systems analyst or a consultant and getting the approval of the person next higher in command for the solving of the problem because commitment to solving the problem (not necessarily just to automation) is essential.

Many libraries lack detailed information about their manual operations so an analysis of present operations and describing in detail the relationships among the parts becomes essential.[62] Throughout the literature and from responses to the survey the point is frequently made that few libraries know enough about this aspect.

After analysis, a synthesis of the alternative solutions should be made.[63] This calls upon the creative competencies of the librarians involved as each remembers the problems to be solved and the desired improvements. At this point reinforcement should be made that more than merely performing the old tasks more quickly and economically will be necessary. A totally new way of doing things is likely to evolve.

Evaluation of the alternatives, according to Boss, means defining the criteria and specifications in terms of expected performance.[64] These criteria and specifications should be based on local needs rather than on a consultant's report alone or on the criteria set by another library or a vendor. Requirements should be grouped and weighed according to priorities which have been determined earlier. Richard W. Meyer sees evaluation as including the ability to screen out the unsuitable candidates against general requirements, evaluating those candidate systems that are left, listing the costs for each system, summarizing, comparing, and choosing.[65] It may be necessary to iterate the steps to increase the detail and modify the results if they do not adequately solve the problem.

Among the planning projects reported in the survey were for: retrospective conversion; the development of acquisition control systems; online catalogs; authority control systems; three libraries planning an automated circulation system which would eventually become an online union catalog; cooperative automated film booking; work flow rearrangements; computer linkage to the commercial bindery; and use of terminals.

But the manager must also plan for implementation which includes the ability to consult with vendors, write performance specifications and contracts, arrange for preparation of sites, prepare and train the staff, convert the data, draft work procedures, and sell the program. Not to be neglected is the manager actually working with the equipment in order to ascertain how the procedures operate, the potential output to expect, and the problems that may occur. Later on the system must be further evaluated. The manager realizes that all this is a risk. As Boss puts it: "Despite a library's best efforts in planning, procurement and promotion, automation can be a failure."[66] And so, among the technical services librarian's competencies must be risk taking, and the abilities to admit failure, bounce back, and start again. S. Michael Malinconico reiterates the same theme in warning that, despite careful planning, uncertainty and risks are not always eliminated; therefore realistic planning allows for unexpected turns of events or fortune such as costs exceeding budgets, time needed for implementation becoming greater than anticipated, or the system failing to perform as expected.[67]

It is a strange quirk of automation that almost at the same time as the technical services librarian plans for a new system, he/she must also plan for obsolescence and make day-to-day decisions about the viability of equipment and systems after they come into use. "The stakes in both situations..." according to Joseph Becker, "are high and the penalties of being surprised by technological change can be severe."[68] This requires more than knowing just how one system works and calls for an intellectual framework for evaluating the emerging technologies in order to place new developments and trends in context with the older ones. Becker describes this as acquiring "a broad, conceptual appreciation of new information technology and an intellectual curiosity about its capabilities, implications and consequences"[69]—competencies which technical services personnel must certainly possess in the 1980s.

Financial Management

Financial managing also takes on new dimensions with application of the new technology. Reductions in staff, often predicted, do not seem to materialize especially during transition times. Margaret Myers agrees with this when she writes: "There is little data on whether automation has resulted in staff cuts. Some librarians have reported on reduction in staff requirements in certain departments, but the total number of library workers has not been radically affected"[70]—although she readily admits that roles and responsibilities and even positions change because of the new technologies. Others speak, in both the literature and in the survey responses, of the staff time required for planning, developing and implementing the new systems and in keeping them going (often, for a time, along with the old systems). Duties expected to diminish, frequently actually increase as Carolynne Myall noted in her response to the survey: "The use of the Virginia Tech Library System and the growth of our collection and services created a need for greater quality control in cataloging and processing. Hence, we now have greater rather than less professional participation in cataloging and processing."[71]

Paul M. Gherman points out a number of considerations that must be taken into account for competent financial management with the new technologies. First of all, if there are reductions in staff, such reductions are likely to occur at the lower end of the salary scale where employees perform routine and repetitive tasks that a machine can do more easily.[72] For those former typists who now work with computer input (e.g., into a bibliographic utility), Gherman notes that, "the complexity of the work has moved upwards considerably along with the pay classification."[73] Planning, budgeting and recruiting must be done for adequately trained (or retrained) staff to do each task. As the nature of work shifts and is no longer just production work, so shifts the demands of the workers. As paraprofessionals take on some of the work previously performed by professional catalogers, their salary expectations rise and all the while the new technologies must be developed and maintained. The new microcomputer may not come with appropriate software and thus programmers are required although none may presently be on the staff.

Gherman further points out that while direct costs for typists to create catalog cards are no longer needed, other personnel such as systems analysts and a greater number of managers will be necessary.[74] If book acquisitions were to drop, typists might be laid off but one cannot lay off technology which must be maintained at the same level regardless of the acquisition level.

Costs for procuring or renting terminals and for telecommunication must be absorbed somewhere in these days of financial retrenchment as well as costs for use of the bibliographic utilities. Thus, we are reminded that technology operates not just within the sphere of the local library but is now a part of networks and bibliographic systems. As Allen Veaner has wisely written:

> In a network one no longer sets one's own priorities. One is part of a group schedule. Decisions made by the group can have significant impact on local planning and budgets. A software change made by a computer manufacturer can require a user to buy new equipment even though the equipment in place is not worn out or obsolete. Changes in hardware can have the same effect. One expected result may be that money destined for an important local program may have to be allocated to maintaining the new technologicall-based [sic] system. And there will be no choice because once installed, it is virtually impossible to revert to the manual system—not even the same forms will be used and if any time has elapsed there may be no one on the staff who remembers enough of the old system to use it.[75]

Gherman concurs: "Participants of these systems can no longer act or exist independently as they once did but they must comply with national codes and standards. Change at the national level therefore means implementation at the local level, whatever the personnel costs."[76] This comes as no great surprise to anyone who has been through the implementation of AACR2, and the OCLC and MARC changes that went along with AACR2 and the establishment of authority files in order to enter data into bibliographic utility databases. These examples could be multiplied many times over by citing changes made by vendors, changes in software development, etc.

Organizational Management

The technical services librarian cannot be satisfied with old methods of organization. It soon becomes obvious that the traditional lines of work patterns no longer function when the new technologies arrive. Old lines of demarcation now result in redundant operations which can be better served by combining acquisition, cataloging and circulation functions. When all services use the same central record, the separate functions blur and overlap. Technical and public services overlap, too, in integrated systems and old barriers must break away—old rivalries cease. This, too, does not come without its birth pangs and death gasps but the competencies of the skillful persons involved help them happen more easily.

People

> The new technologies are changing the inner workings of the library. The automated systems are important in facilitating the workload but our human resources are still our strongest asset and they need to be thoughtfully and carefully supported through the changes brought about by automated systems. When the systems are fully in place, they will only be as good as the people who interact with them.

So responded Marie Kaskus[77] to the technical services survey while another respondent, James Chervinko, noted that:

> Despite all the wonders and problems of automation, technical services is still a people organization. The computers are simply tools—in the real sense....Above all, it is the people in technical services, the administrators, librarians, paraprofessionals, and clerical workers, who have to decide how best to use automation in their operation.[78]

In writing about serials staffing guidelines for the 1980s, Margaret McKinley speaks out of long experience in saying: "Automation, the optimists' great hope and the pessimists' great fear, depends heavily for its success on an enthusiastic staff, carefully prepared for the radical changes which automation brings in its wake."[79] These three persons attest to the necessity for yet another important competency—the skillful management of change in relation to people. Everyone fears change and although most of us are better able to cope with the changes brought about by computers than we were a few years ago, even today there is still likely to be an element of fear, and especially of inadequacy, when *your* job becomes affected by the computer. A computer system requires different mental and emotional skills to work with it than does a manual system. For example, a computer system frequently demands more abstract thinking than does a manual system while at the same time the computer system requires a conformity and adherence to its protocols, delays and down times, and a tolerance of its blatant intolerance of errors or even slight deviations from its procedures. All of this may be difficult for some people to accept.

Nothing will be quite the same again when the computer comes to stay. It is a bittersweet experience full of anticipation yet mixed with a bit of sadness knowing that old work relationships and procedures will certainly change. Each staff member should be prepared for this change in relationships just as my mother tried to tell me before my marriage that our close family relationship would never again be quite the same. I argued and disputed her wisdom—but she *was* right. There were tradeoffs, of course, but you can never "go home again" in quite the same way. Technical services staff should be made aware of the changes in relationships that come with the introduction of a new "family member" when the "bridegroom" is a computer. Zuboff says it this way:

New forms of technology inevitably change the ways people are mobil-
ized to work as well as the kinds of skills and behavior that are critical for
productivity. These changes are rarely born without pain and conflict—
nor do they emerge exactly as planners envision them. Instead, new
conceptions of work organization and behavior emerge from an interaction between the demands of a new technology, its social organization,
and the responses of the men and women who must work with the new
technological system.[80]

In my technical services seminar, we use a role playing experience to
emphasize the problems associated with change—in this case change that
results from the installation of OCLC into a medical school's library. This
note appears in the in-basket of the technical services librarian:

> For the past several months, I have been working at least six hours per
> day at the OCLC terminal while we are putting forth an all-out effort to
> input our new holdings and do some retrospective conversion especially
> of our serials holdings in anticipation of using the OCLC Serials Subsys-
> tem. As you know, we have only one terminal and therefore the two of us
> who work with the project are scheduled for different hours. We drew lots
> and I drew the afternoon shift working until OCLC "goes down" in the
> evening.
>
> I am writing you this note because I think that OCLC is affecting my
> health. Lately my eyes have been bothering me a lot. I can no longer focus
> for long periods of time. I see colored fringes around objects and often my
> vision is blurred. I am using up my salary buying eye drops. I have heard
> of people turning "green with envy," well, I am turning green from
> seeing those OCLC letters for so many hours a day. Even at night when I
> go home, and close my eyes, it seems as if I still see those green letters
> floating around.
>
> I really used to like my job and the people I worked with. Now I am
> beginning to hate it. First of all, I really miss my friends that I worked
> with. I enjoyed them so much as we shared work and life's little experien-
> ces. Now, I seldom see some of them. All I have to talk to is the
> computer—and it doesn't care one bit (or for that matter, byte) about me
> and the things that matter to me. Sometimes I feel like a slave chained to a
> galley—my galley is the terminal. And those chairs we have for the
> terminal really don't fit me—my feet don't touch the floor and I am
> getting a crick in my neck all the time—and a backache as well!
>
> But at least I don't wear bifocals—then my neck really would hurt!
> And talk about frustrations—those really *come* when the system goes
> down—how I hate just sitting there (like a captive) waiting for that dumb
> machine to get its act together. And since it is rather quiet around here in
> the evenings when I work, it gets lonely waiting for those people in
> Columbus, Dublin, or wherever they are in Ohio now, to fix whatever is
> wrong or to enhance or whatever they are doing on MY time and making
> me lose MY statistics. (By the way, I might as well tell you that rumor has
> it that you are basing our merit raises upon our statistics at the
> terminal—in some ways, I don't think that is fair—I don't have any
> control over what happens as far as downtime is concerned. I just wanted
> you to know my sentiments about this while I am getting things off my
> mind and down on paper.)

Another thing that bothers me is when there is trouble with the terminal, and I become one of the 3000 calls a week OCLC says it gets at the User Services.[81] That's a statistic I'd rather not be—talking to an engineer five hundred miles away who expects me to know what a cable is and where it leads to and whether a plug is male or female is not my idea of chatty conversation on the phone.

And then there are the times we have to wait for Paradyne from Peoria to come over and repair the modem—only to find the next day that that whatever thing isn't even plugged into the modem. I was never cut out to work with this kind of stuff. Add to this the fact that I'm missing out on a lot of social life because of my strange work hours and I think you'll see why I am feeling depressed and dissatisfied and find myself worrying all the time. Lately, I have found yet a new worry—concern about the harmful effects to my health from the radiation from the terminal— working with all this medical stuff does tend to open one's mind to the powers of suggestion! Recently, on my 15 minute break per half day (or night), I started reading up on harmful effects to our environment and, believe me, I am beginning to think that working at a CRT is high on the charts for that! Do you think maybe I'm experiencing burnout?

It is not too farfetched to believe that such a letter could have appeared in any number of real in-baskets (indeed, there is literature[82] that speaks to these problems and each aspect was mentioned at least once by the librarians responding to the survey completed prior to the preparation of this paper). Wise is the librarian who, as Malinconico[83] suggests, both "hears" and "listens" to the resistance to change; wiser yet is the librarian who exerts a leadership role and who motivates the staff to develop positive attitudes toward change by skillful involvement of each person of any rank in the change process.

Sara Fine reports on a nationwide study that she has conducted among library administrators, practicing public librarians, library master's students, and library school faculty in which the findings have confirmed that the thing people fear most about the new technologies is that interpersonal relationships will suffer. However, the findings also indicate "that resistance is related to whether or not people are a part of the decision-making process in their organization."[84] By working with the staff to help them understand what *may* happen and by being sensitized to the harmful effects—physical and psychological—that may occur and cause stress, much resistance can be countered. Necks do get stiff; bi- and tri-focal wearers do experience difficulties and few work stations seem to have been designed with even a modicum of comfort in mind. Workers do take pride in their jobs—sometimes becoming even a bit proprietary about them— and when the alignments and working relationships are challenged, humans do tend to act as humans. Perhaps this has been the most difficult problem for catalogers for many of their duties have now, with the library networks, been taken over by support staff. (This was by far the area cited most frequently as having been changed by those who responded to the survey.) There are catalogers who really do like to catalog—and as the professional cataloger is removed to managerial and supervisory responsibilities, that person may find these new duties less satisfying to him or her. And some help may be needed to make the transition easier.

Whatever the position, the person who does not like change (not necessarily related to chronological age) will not easily cope with the consistency with which the new technologies spawn change. Eventually automation does bring about changes in organizational patterns in libraries—catalog departments may no longer exist as centralized entities; circulation departments leave public services for technical services; technical services are no longer even known by that name. Supervisors are changed. Workers who formerly shared the same work areas are now found on different floors of the building. The pride once felt for following a task through to completion and holding a completed product in one's hand is swallowed up into an intangible grey terminal and probably, for all the workers know, digested by some Pac Man-like creature. No longer does the worker feel like a real "craftsperson." Malinconico suggests that the transition period from one system to another should not be rushed, particularly if it differs radically from the new one and he quotes David Nadler of the Columbia University School of Business, who says that: "People need to mourn for the old system or familiar way of doing things. This is frequently manifested in the emergence of stories or myths about the 'good old days,' even when those days weren't so good. The process of dealing with loss takes time, and those managing change should take this into account."[85]

It becomes obvious that sympathy, compassion, motivation, understanding, a sense of good timing, and leadership become an important part of the competency pack for the technical services supervisor at this juncture as does the ability to recognize who is right for a particular job, realign existing staff and recruit new staff members from a variety of backgrounds.

The communication capabilities and competencies of the technical services librarian reach out to many different groups of people in dealing with the new technologies. In addition to close staff relationships within the local library, one will be working with persons outside the library; some of whom were not even mentioned in library school: engineers, electricians, telephone and other communications personnel, computer programmers, systems analysts, consultants, vendors, network service personnel, and those who work in the networks as well. Frequently automation work is teamwork or is a task force assignment involving many levels of personnel from all areas of the library, from different sectors of the local environment, and from many areas of expertise. Some of these persons do not speak "bibliographic recordese" and the ability to speak in their terms can be a real benefit.

In a network environment, control of the local environment is no longer truly local—much depends upon communication not only with persons but with machines far, far away. Vendors, engineers, personnel at network service centers and in users' councils, as well as those who form the governing bodies of networks influence our local operations and take our time and money more than we frequently care to admit.[86] And we—often to our dismay—need to become political in communicating with them and making our own needs and wishes known—and in resolving new and recurring issues of who owns the records, of copyright, etc.

Administrators and top management must know about our needs and plans. Communication is often, especially in special libraries, with administrators who have little knowledge of library needs. Today local automation projects frequently involve several libraries—particularly in the school and public library sector—and special negotiation skills must be developed in order to determine one standard for several libraries that have been doing things differently.

Users, too, need to be among the communication chain as it is prudent to make them aware of impending changes—and why there will be changes. Public relations at this juncture is very important to help assure acceptance of the change.

Clearly written communications are as much a necessity as are oral ones. Well-defined specifications, requests for proposals (RFP), work procedures, manuals, routines, and contracts have to be prepared as does other documentation. Because the new technologies continue to change, all of this will likely need to be done over and over again. No one system is apt to be satisfactory for long as the new technology of yesterday becomes the middle-aged technology of today and the geriatric technology of tomorrow. Patience and fortitude pay off in the communication arena but one also learns to defend one's own position. As Keith Trimmer put it in his survey response: "You can't be afraid to say 'This is unacceptable.' "[87] But one also learns to compromise and to eventually accept "tradeoffs."

Increasingly those who work in technical services must develop (or redevelop) the competencies of both a learner and a teacher, because as Constance L. Etter pointed out in the survey, "the moderate mushrooming of new technologies, new services, companies, devices, etc. just means that there is *much more* to learn about and try to keep abreast of *beyond* acquiring and maintaining good traditional library skills."[88] As a learner, he/she must be skillful in reading and interpreting technical information, in understanding new developments, in learning about areas which do not fit into the usual humanities and social science backgrounds from which many librarians came. Materials in disciplines and subdisciplines of the classification scheme which previously had been encountered only in acquiring, cataloging or binding these materials now become regular reading matter. Each week's run of mail brings news of conferences where attendance must be considered relating to online systems, authority control, cooperation, microcomputers, and management. Telephones and electronic mail convey help from colleagues. Courses are enrolled in. Workshops, offered by associations, networks, consortia, and educational institutions, are attended as well as those given by vendors and user groups. Eventually the technical services librarian takes his/her place as a teacher and passes on what has been learned to others by teaching the public services librarian to learn about the RLIN system as a reference tool, the cataloger to interact with the vendor-supplied acquisition system, and the acquisition librarian to use the automated serial check-in system. Frequently, the paraprofessional now engaged in online cataloging has not had the opportunity to acquire a library school education. The librarian becomes the educator—conveying the purposes, objectives and functions of building a catalog as well as the required technical knowledge for adapting or making bibliographic records in the new system.

Teaching is not just confined to the library staff. Users will have to learn to use the new catalogs and other tools. Innovative techniques both from the traditional and technological environments will be employed to teach users how to effectively utilize the new tools. Users with their own microcomputers will work outside the traditional library setting to gain bibliographic access—they cannot ask their questions face-to-face—the new tools must make use of new instructional means and software packages to instruct the users.

SUMMARY

To fulfill the functions of the technical services, now, as never before, persons are needed who are dedicated to the service of library users. To do this, they need bibliographic and technical skills to assist them in acquiring materials, in making the tools that organize the collections and in providing the means to preserve them. Thinkers (with analytical minds) problem solvers, decision makers, and leaders are a necessity! These persons must be inquisitive, curious, imaginative, and creative—they must be capable of managing, organizing, supervising, and communicating. And, at this particular time, the message that comes through is that they should be adaptable and flexible persons amenable to change—as well as dreamers that envision new and better tools as the means to better service for users. Through all of this they must retain their sense of purpose—and sense of humor.

Over and over again the respondents to the survey noted how change had affected the technical services environment even within the short span of five to ten years. Even in their wildest imagination, some confessed, they could not have believed the activities they would be engaged in today. But changes are not over yet. We all know that. Eloise Vondruska, one of the respondents to the survey, spoke for all of us when she wrote:

> Today I have to be familiar with library applications of microcomputers as we prepare for a crop of Apples next year. But there were no Apples when I was in school ten years ago. I cannot venture to know what will be on the menu in another 10 years. But I do know that I will still need to be flexible, open to change and able to analyze problems, the competencies I listed first.[89]

If we all have such insatiable appetites, the functions of the technical services, regardless of how they are organized or by what name they are known, will fulfill the vision Randall had for them almost a half century ago. I am sure that he, like most of us, would be surprised by the turn many of these "most typical of library activities" have taken, but I believe that he would be happy and excited by the potential for services which lie ahead and that he would be somewhat envious of the opportunity afforded those persons who possess the many required competencies to carry out such services in the future.

REFERENCES

1. Randall, William M. "The Technical Processes and Library Service." In *The Acquisition and Cataloging of Books* (Library Institute, University of Chicago, Graduate Library School), edited by William M. Randall, p. 1. Chicago: The University of Chicago Press, 1940.

2. "Bulletin Board: Positions Available." *The Chronicle of Higher Education* 25(Sept.-Dec. 1982).

3. *LJ/SLJ Hotline*. Sept.-Dec. 1982.

4. Janet S. Huettner assisted by S. Elaine Stokes helped in the identification and coding of the data. Ms. Huettner developed a computer program to compile the statistics and to avoid duplication of the announcements. Both Ms. Huettner and Ms. Stokes are recent graduates of the Graduate School of Library and Information Science (GSLIS), University of Illinois at Urbana-Champaign (UIUC) and both are currently employed at the Purdue University Libraries.

5. Only those persons quoted directly or who contributed unique ideas will be identified by name; however, the ideas of each respondent are in some way incorporated into this paper.

6. Richard A. Stewart to Kathryn Luther Henderson, personal communication, 18 March March 1983. Stewart is a graduate of the University of Chicago Graduate Library School. He responded to the survey at the suggestion of a GSLIS, UIUC graduate who had received the survey form.

7. Keith Russell to Kathryn Luther Henderson, personal communication, 4 April 1983.

8. Randall, "The Technical Processes and Library Service," p. 13.

9. McDermott, Judy C., "New Challenges for Library Acquisitions." *Journal of Library Administration* 3(Summer 1982):1.

10. Ibid., p. 2.

11. Ibid., p. 3.

12. Hickey, Thomas B. "The Journal in the Year 2000." In *Serials Management in an Automated Age* (Serials Conference: 1981), edited by Nancy Jean Melin, pp. 7-8. Westport, Conn.: Meckler Publications, 1982.

13. "ACS Journals to be Available On-Line." *Chemical & Engineering News* 61(11 April 1983):7-8.

14. Bearman, Toni Carbo. "The Impact of Technology on Libraries: Opening Commentary." In *Information Technology: Critical Choices for Library Decision-Makers* (Books in Library and Information Science, vol. 40), edited by Allen Kent and Thomas J. Galvin, p. 37. New York: Marcel Dekker, 1982.

15. For two recent articles offering help in this area see, Emard, Jean-Paul. "Software Hang-ups and Glitches: Problems to be Faced & Overcome." *Online* 7(Jan. 1983):18-23; and Mason, Robert M. "Searching for Software: Finding & Buying the 'Right Stuff.' " *Library Journal* 108(15 April 1983):801-02.

16. *Anglo-American Cataloguing Rules*, 2d ed., edited by Michael Gorman and Paul W. Winkler. Chicago: ALA, 1978.

17. Ibid., pp. 201-16.

18. Dodd, Sue A. *Cataloging Machine-Readable Data Files: An Interpretive Manual.* Chicago: ALA, 1982.

19. Emard, "Software Hang-ups and Glitches," pp. 21-22.

20. Ibid., p. 22.

21. Matthews, Joseph R. "The Automated Library System Marketplace, 1982: Change and More Change." *Library Journal* 108(15 March 1983):547-53. Matthews discusses the increasing availability of automated library systems including those available for acquisitions.

22. Reid, Marion T. "Effectiveness of the OCLC Data Base for Acquisitions Verification." *Journal of Academic Librarianship* 2(Jan. 1977):303, 306.

23. Several studies have been made of the optimum time to search and re-search the On-line Computer Library Center (OCLC) database such as: Metz, Paul, and Espley, John. "The Availability of Cataloging Copy in the OCLC Data Base." *College & Research Libraries* 41(Sept. 1980):430-36; and McDonough, Joyce C., et al. "Moving the Backlog an Optimum Cycle for Searching OCLC." *Library Acquisitions: Practice and Theory* 6(1982):265-70.

24. A helpful guide to choosing the best search key for a particular search on OCLC was distributed with OCLC materials from the ILLINET network early in 1983: See Rohdy, Margaret A. "Are You Searching Efficiently? A Guide to Search Strategy." Springfield, Ill., Illinois State Library, 1983 (included are guidelines for choosing the most efficient search key and use of qualifiers).

25. *Books in Print.* New York: Bowker.

26. *Ulrich's International Periodicals Directory.* New York: Bowker.

27. Uszak, Andy. "Bowker Goes Online." *Technicalities* 2(Jan. 1982):11, 15.

28. *Anglo-American Cataloging Rules* (North American ed.). Chicago: ALA, 1967.

29. OCLC, Inc. *Acquisitions: User Manual.* Dublin, Ohio: OCLC, 1981, p. 5, 32.

30. *MARC Formats for Bibliographic Data.* Washington, D.C.: Library of Congress, Automated Systems Office, 1980.

31. American National Standards Institute. *American National Standard for Serial Holdings Statements at the Summary Level* (ANSI Z39.42-1980). New York: ANSI, 1980; and Wittorf, Robert. "ANSI Z39.42 and OCLC: OCLC's Implementation of the American National Standard Institute's Serial Holdings Statements at the Summary Level." *Serials Review* 6(April/June 1980):87.

32. Bruns, Phyllis A. *National Level Bibliographic Record–Books.* Washington: Library of Congress, 1980 (NLBRs for other formats have been prepared or are being prepared).

33. The Library of Congres Rule Interpretations appear in *Cataloging Service Bulletin.* Washington, D.C.: Library of Congress, Processing Services (beginning with no. 11, Winter 1981).

34. Younger, Jennifer. "Cooperative Name Authority Project" from *Authorities: Persons, Corporate Bodies & Series.* Tapes from the 100th Annual American Library Association Conference, San Francisco, California, June 1981. Tape 81107-342.

35. Statement made by President Richard W. McCoy, RLG, Inc. (Research Libraries Group) at "Networking: Where from Here?" a conference held at Champaign, Illinois, 12 April 1983.

36. Davison, Wayne E. "The WLN/RLG/LC Linked Systems Project." *Information Technology and Libraries* 2(March 1983):34.

37. "Preliminary *Authority Record* is Now Available from CDS." *Library of Congress Information Bulletin* 42(7 March 1983):89-90.

38. Hickey, Thomas B., and Spies, Phyllis B. "Standards for Information Display." *Library Trends* 31(Fall 1982):316.

39. "Utilities Agree to Use BISAC Order Format." *American Libraries* 14(March 1982):197.

40. Ibid.

41. "Semiannual Report on Developments at the Library of Congress April 1, 1982, through September 30, 1982." *Library of Congress Information Bulletin* 41(20 Dec. 1982):424. (In response to a question asked at the "'Blood, Toil, Tears and Sweat': Rules and Formats" institute sponsored by the Resources and Technical Services Division, Cataloging and Classification Section at the American Library Association's conference on 28 June 1983, Henriette D. Avram indicated that UNIMARC is intended for use only between national bibliographic centers and will be used by the Library of Congress only on an international basis.)

42. Ayres, F.H., et al. "The USBC and Control of the Bibliographic Database." *Information Technology and Libraries* 1(March 1982):44-45.

43. *IDP Report* (18 Feb. 1983):6; and *LJ/SLJ Hotline* 12(13 June 1983):6.

44. Cochrane, Pauline A. "Can a Standard for an Online Common Command Language be Developed?" *Online* 7(Jan. 1983):36-37.

45. Zuboff, Shoshana, "New Worlds of Computer-Mediated Work." *Harvard Business Review* 60(Sept.-Oct. 1982):146. (Zuboff is an Assistant Professor of Organizational Behavior and Human Resource Management at the Harvard Business School.)

46. Sara Stephan Clapp to Kathryn Luther Henderson, personal communication, 21 March 1983.

47. Freedman, Mitch. "A Conversation with Frederick G. Kilgour." *Technicalities* 1(June 1981):3.

48. Carter, Nancy F. "Suggestions for the Teaching of Cataloging." *Technicalities* 3(April 1983):12.

49. Hildreth, Charles R. *Online Public Access Catalogs: The User Interface* (OCLC Library, Information, and Computer Services Series). Dublin, Ohio: OCLC, 1982.

50. Salmon, Stephen R. "Characteristics of Online Public Catalogs." *Library Resources & Technical Services* 27(Jan./March 1983):36-67.

51. Matthews, Joseph R. *Public Access to Online Catalogs: A Planning Guide for Managers*. Weston, Conn.: Online, Inc. 1982.

52. "In-Depth: University of California MELVYL." *Information Technology and Libraries* 1(Dec. 1982):350-80; and 2(March 1983):58-115.

53. Besant, Larry. "Users of Public Online Catalogs Want Sophisticated Subject Access." *American Libraries* 14(March 1982):160; *Online Catalogs: Requirements, Characteristics and Costs* (Report of a Conference Sponsored by the Council on Library Resources at Aspen Institute, Wye Plantation, Queenstown, Md., 14-16 Dec. 1982), edited by Davis B. McCarn. Washington, D.C.: Council on Library Resources, 1983, pp. 8, 10, 18, 21; and Kaske, Neal K., and Sanders, Nancy P. *A Comprehensive Study of Online Public Access Catalogs: An Overview and Application of Findings* (Final Report to the Council on Library Resources, vol. 3) (Report Number: OCLC/OPR/RR-83/4). Dublin, Ohio: OCLC, Inc., 31 March 1983, p. 51.

54. DeGennaro, Richard. "Library Automation & Networking Perspectives on Three Decades." *Library Journal* 108(1 April 1983):633.

55. William T Henderson, Binding and Preservation Librarian, University of Illinois at Urbana-Champaign assisted in the preparation of this section.

56. Gibson, Gerald D. "Preservation of Nonpaper Materials: Present and Future Research and Development in the Preservation of Film, Sound Recordings, Tapes, Computer Records, and Other Nonpaper Materials." In *Conserving and Preserving Library Materials* (Proceedings of the 1981 Allerton Park Institute, no. 27), edited by Kathryn Luther Henderson and William T Henderson, p. 105. Urbana-Champaign: University of Illinois, Graduate School of Library and Information Science, 1983. Among the problems identified are unknowns concerning its potential life, its susceptibility to fluctuation in heat and humidity, discoloration with age, and separability of the laminated "sandwich" which makes up the disk as well as the fact that "the present state of [the] video does not allow for direct retrieval of an image with enough clarity and definition for most motion picture researchers, much less for the specialist working with manuscripts, art or maps, to name but three fields dependent upon clarity and resolution of image."

57. Sonnemann, Sabine S. "The Videodisc as a Library Tool." *Special Libraries* 74(Jan. 1983):7.

58. "LC Awards Contracts for Optical Disk Technology." *Wilson Library Bulletin* 57(Jan. 1983):376.

59. Statement made by Richard W. McCoy at "Networking: Where from Here?" conference, 12 April 1983.

60. Statement made by Frank P. Grisham, Executive Director of SOLINET (Southeastern Library Network) at "Networking: Where from Here?" a conference held at Champaign, Illinois, 12 April 1983.

61. Boss, Richard W. *The Library Manager's Guide to Automation* (Professional Librarian Series). White Plains, N.Y.: Knowledge Industry Publications, Inc., 1979, p. 46. (Boss acknowledges that he originally obtained and expanded upon these steps from Robert S. Taylor and Caroline Hieber's *Manual for the Analysis of Library Systems*. Bethlehem, Pa.: Lehigh University, 1965.)

62. Ibid., pp. 46-47.

63. Ibid., pp. 47-48.

64. Ibid., p. 48.

65. Meyer, Richard W. "A Methodology and Linear Model for System Planning and Evaluation." *Cause/Effect* 5(Nov. 1982):15.

66. Boss, *The Library Manager's Guide to Automation*, p. 61.

67. Malinconico, S. Michael. "Planning for Failure." *Library Journal* 108(15 April 1983):798.

68. Becker, Joseph. "How to Integrate and Manage New Technology in the Library." *Special Libraries* 74(Jan. 1983):4.

69. Ibid.

70. Myers, Margaret. "Staffing Patterns in Libraries." In *Personnel Administration in Libraries*, edited by Sheila Creth and Frederick Duda, p. 48. New York: Neal-Schuman, 1981.

71. Carolynne Myall to Kathryn Luther Henderson, personal communication, 21 March 1983.

72. Gherman, Paul M. "Salary Planning." *Journal of Library Administration* vol. 3, nos. 3 and 4, Fall/Winter 1982, p. 94.

73. Ibid., p. 95.

74. Ibid., p. 94.

75. Veaner, Allen B. "Management and Technology." *IFLA Journal* 7(1981):34.

76. Gherman, "Salary Planning," p. 95.

77. Marie Kascus to Kathryn Luther Henderson, personal communication, 12 March 1983.

78. James Chervinko to Kathryn Luther Henderson, personal communication, 14 March 1983.

79. McKinley, Margaret. "Serials Staffing Guidlines for the 80's." In *The Serials Collection: Organization and Administration* (Current Issues in Serials Management No. 1), edited by Nancy Jean Melin, p. 36. Ann Arbor, Mich.: Pierian Press, 1982.

80. Zuboff, "New Worlds of Computer-Mediated Work," p.143.

81. OCLC. 19 March 1983. This statistic came from the OCLC screen for 19 March 1983, the second anniversary of the User Services.

82. See, for example, Zuboff, "New Worlds of Computer-Mediated Work"; Biggs, Mary. "Resistance to Change." *Resource Sharing & Library Networks* 1(Winter 1981/Spring 1982):3-23; McDermott, Judy C. "Is OCLC Dangerous to Your Health?" *Journal of Library Administration* 2(Spring 1981):7-11; and Alley, Brian. "What You Can't See...a Conversation with Charles Wallach." *Technicalities* 2(Nov. 1982):1, 3-4.

83. Malinconico, S. Michael. "Hearing the Resistance." *Library Journal* 108(15 Jan. 1983):111-13; and "Listening to the Resistance." *Library Journal* 108(15 Feb. 1983):353-55.

84. Fine, Sara. "Human Factors and Human Consequences: Opening Commentary." In *Information Technology: Critical Choices for Library Decision-Makers*, p. 213.

85. Nadler, David A. *Concepts for the Management of Organizational Change.* New York: OR&C Consultants, Inc., 1980, p. 6 (as quoted by Malinconico, "Planning for Failure," p. 800).

86. Articles which speak to some of these relationships in regard to governance include: Boykin, Joseph F., Jr., and Walbridge, Sharon. "The OCLC Users Council." *Resource Sharing & Library Networks* 1(Winter 1981/Spring 1982):51-65; Bruntjen, Scott. "The Political, Economic, and Technological Roots of Some Legal Issues in Library Networking." *Journal of Library Administration* 3(Summer 1982):15-27; Carlile, Huntington, and Burkley, John H. "Legal Aspects of Organizing a Library Network." *Bulletin of the American Society for Information Science* 6(June 1980):16-18; Galvin, Thomas J. "Library Networks—Trends and Issues in Evaluation and Governance." *Illinois Libraries* 62(April 1980):289-93; Jones, Robert E. "The Recent Transformation of WLN Governance." *Resource Sharing & Library Networks* 1(Winter/Spring 1982):67-84; and Riddick, John F. "The OCLC Union List Group: The Agent-Client Relationship." *Technicalities* 3(Feb. 1983):5-6.

87. Keith Trimmer to Kathryn Luther Henderson, personal communication, 19 March 1983.

88. Constance Etter to Kathryn Luther Henderson, personal communication, 14 March 1983.

89. Eloise Vondruska to Kathryn Luther Henderson, personal communication, 21 March 1983.

ADDITIONAL REFERENCES

Adcock, Donald C. "Into the '80s: An Overview of the Future of Technical Services in the School Library." *Illinois Libraries* 62(Sept. 1980):592-94.

Asheim, Lester. "Education of Future Academic Librarians." In *Adacemic Libraries by the Year 2000*, edited by Herbert Poole, pp. 128-38. New York: R.R. Bowker, 1977.

Avram, Henriette D. "Network-Level Decisions: Basis and Key Issues." *Resource Sharing & Library Networks* 1(Winter 1981/Spring 1982):91-100.

Battin, Patricia. "Developing University and Research Library Professionals: A Director's Perspective." *American Libraries* 14(Jan. 1983):22-24.

Brown, Thomas M. "Technical Services in the 1980s in School Libraries: Trends and Problems." *Illinois Libraries* 62(Sept. 1980):594-96.

Clarkson, Sara H., and Zecher—Tropp, Freda. "Education for Technical Service Librarians." *Technicalities* 2(Oct. 1982):6,13-14.

Conroy, Barbara. "The Human Element: Staff Development in the Electronic Library." *Drexel Library Quarterly* 17(Fall 1981):91-106.

Corey, James F., et al. "Involving Faculty and Students in the Selection of a Catalog Alternative." *Journal of Academic Librarianship* 8(Jan. 1983):328-33.

Cuadra, Carlos A. "A Brief Introduction to Electronic Publishing." *Electronic Publishing Review* 1(March 1981):29-42.

Dowlin, C. Edwin. "Education for the Electronic Library." *Drexel Library Quarterly* 17(Fall 1981):77-90.

Dumont, Paul E. "The Technician Facing Change: The Use of the Computer in Technical Services." *COLT Newsletter* 13(March 1980):1-4.

Edge, Sharon M. "Options in Technology: Academic Libraries, April 1st and 2nd, 1982: The LAPT Report: A Study in Contrasts?" *Library Acquisitions: Practice and Theory* 6(1982): 271-88.

Funk, Carla. "By Any Name: The Future of Technical Services in the Small and Medium-Sized Libraries." *Illinois Libraries* 62(Sept. 1980):590-92.

Ghikas, Mary W. "Technical Services in the '80s: Challenge and Change." *Illinois Libraries* 62(Sept. 1980):588-90.

Gorman, Michael. "Technical Services in an Automated Library." In *The Role of the Library in an Electronic Society* (Proceedings of the 1979 Clinic on Library Applications of Data Processing), edited by F. Wilfrid Lancaster, pp. 48-59. Urbana-Champaign: University of Illinois Graduate School of Library and Information Science, 1980.

Hanson, Jo Ann. "A Model for Organization of the Automated Academic Library." *Technicalities* 2(Oct. 1982):7-8.

Horny, Karen L. "Technical Services Librarians: A Vanishing Species." *Illinois Libraries* 62(Sept. 1980):587-88.

Hurowitz, Robert, and McDonald, David R. "Library Automation and Library Organization: An Analysis of Future Trends." In *Options for the 80s. Part B* (Association of College and Research Libraries National Conference: 1981) (Foundations in Library and Information Science Series, vol. 17), edited by Michael D. Kathman and Virgil F. Massman, pp. 613-20. Greenwich, Conn.: JAI Press, 1982.

Kaske, Neal K., and Sanders, Nancy P. "Networking and the Electronic Library." *Drexel Library Quarterly* 17(Fall 1981):65-76.

Kennedy, Gail. "Technical Processing Librarians in the 1980s: Current Trends and Future Forecasts" (University of Kentucky Libraries. Occasional Papers, vol. 1, no. 1, Aug. 1980).

Lancaster, F. Wilfrid. *Libraries and Librarians in an Age of Electronics.* Arlington, Va.: Information Resources Press,1982.

Lin, Nan, and Zaltman, Gerald. "Dimensions of Innovation." In *Processes and Phenomena of Social Change*, edited by Gerald Zaltman et al., pp. 93-115. New York: John Wiley, 1973.

Marchant, Maurice P., and Smith, Nathan M. "The Research Library Director's View of Library Education." *College & Research Lilbraries* 43(Nov. 1982):437-44.

Matthews, Joseph R. *Choosing an Automated Library System.* Chicago: ALA, 1980.

Microcomputers in Libraries (Applications in Information Management and Technology Series), edited by Ching-chih Chen and Stacey E. Bressler. New York: Neal-Schuman, 1982.

Myers, Margaret. "Library Personnel: Supply and Demand." *Drexel Library Quarterly* 17(Summer 1981):94-117.

Oyler, Patricia G. "Education for Technical Services in the 1980s." *Illinois Libraries* 62(Sept. 1980):596-98.

Rohdy, Margaret A. "The Management of Technical Services—1980." *Library Resources & Technical Services* 25(July/Sept. 1981):319-29.

Sebestyen, Istvan. "The Videodisc Revolution." *Electronic Publishing Review* 2(March 1982):41-89.

Shaughnessy, Thomas W. "Technology and Job Design in Libraries: A Sociotechnical Systems Approach." *Journal of Academic Librarianship* 3(Nov. 1977):269-72.

—————— . "Technology and the Structure of Libraries." *Libri* 32(June 1982):149-55.

Shera, Jesse H. "Mechanization, Librarianship, and the Bibliographic Enterprise." *Journal of Documentation* 30(June 1974):153-69.

Watson, Goodwin. "Resistance to Change." In *Processes and Phenomena of Social Change*, pp. 117-31.

Weber, David C. "Personal Aspects of Library Automation." *Journal of Library Automation* 4(March 1971):27-37.

White, Robert M. "Disk-Storage Technology." *Scientific American* 243(Aug. 1980):138-48.

DANUTA A. NITECKI
Associate Director for Public Services
University of Maryland Libraries

Competencies Required of Public Services Librarians to Use New Technologies

The classic dichotomy within librarianship roughly divides the profession's functions into two—the technical activities of acquiring and organizing recorded information on the one hand and on the other hand the public assistance to interpret and disseminate this stored information. Within this setting, the main function of public services librarians is to help library users to acquire needed information. To do so involves personal interactions, interpretation of needs, retrieval of information, and delivery of documents, facts or directions.

Does the utilization of new technologies which are appearing in libraries demand the development of new competencies among public services librarians to peform their function? Are we in the midst of a revolutionary change whereby "the availability of online bibliographic searching has created demand for librarians with new skills and expertise."[1]

This quote is representative of much of the literature which heralds the arrival of and demand for a new breed of librarian—one equipped with new skills to use the technology. A digestion of some of this literature, however, within the larger framework of what it is that public services librarians do, suggests that most of the identified requirements for successful functioning are identical to earlier expectations. This paper thus proposes that the basic competencies required of public services librarians to perform their primary functions today are the same whether or not automated resources are used. Yet the utilization of such tools has placed a greater focus on the librarian's accountability and perhaps for the near future has increased user dependency. The byproducts may be examined in light of other services provided.

The aim of this paper is to review the competencies required of public services librarians to utilize the new technologies. This review will consist of (1) an identification of basic public services librarians' competencies, (2) a consideration of where the present impact of technologies is most felt within public service activities, and (3) a discussion of how online retrieval technologies have affected the attainment of the basic public services competencies.

Two difficulties with a topic such as this one are that drawn conclusions change dependent on one's time perspective, and that we have various thresholds for mediocrity. My observations are based on my current perceptions of the past and the present. They are also based on a practitioner's experiences and what is undoubtedly not an exhaustive review of the literature. Proposed observations are made based on the present state of technology in libraries. A few speculations concerning future trends and the subsequent effects on public services librarians' competencies will be restricted to the end of this paper.

I had difficulty with the concept of competency itself. My first association with the term *competent* is that it is an evaluative, generally complimentary adjective describing a level of ability engendering trust, confidence and respect of the person demonstrating the competency. And yet the dictionary defines *competence* as adequacy or sufficiency. One who is competent is "adequate but not exceptional." My perspective thus dropped to focus on minimal requirements and not ideals. I agree with José-Marie Griffiths that a base level of basics needs to be recognized and in turn used to qualify requirements to accomplish our tasks and to facilitate design of training programs. However, as a manager of a service requiring the personnel resources of professionals, I aim higher and seek qualities that go beyond minimal requirements. My difficulty however is to express that expectation in measurable terms. Qualities such as service attitude, potential for growth, commitment to common goals, creativeness, and intelligence are indicative of the evasive nature of the topic.

Identification of Public Services Competencies

To accomplish their primary function of linking users to needed information, public services librarians must master various skills. These might be categorized into five basic types of competencies, including the abilities (1) to communicate with others, (2) to analyze needs, (3) to retrieve data, (4) to instruct users, and (5) to manage operations and supervise staff who provide services.

This particular categorization is based on impressions from the limited literature on the topic I was able to identify and from considering the public services activities. The indexed literature was searched online and manually for material on professional competencies and very little was found. In addition, staff of the American Library Association (ALA) Reference and Adult Services Division (RASD) and the Office for Library Personnel Resources were contacted. A search of the ALA Archives was also conducted by staff of the University of Illinois at Urbana-Champaign Library Archives.

An excellent review of the literature prior to 1978 relating to the topic is summarized by Suzanne H. Mahmoodi in her Ph.D. dissertation entitled, "Identification of Competencies for Librarians Performing Public Services Functions in Public Libraries." She describes four approaches taken in the literature: (1) concerns related to library education; (2) design of accreditation, certification or standards to upgrade the profession; (3) differentiation between levels of staffing; and (4) identification of components of a job.[2] Mahmoodi makes several pertinent observations:

> Accrediting library education programs, and establishing qualifications for certification, both of which must reflect the standards specified by professional organizations, for the most part have not focused upon development of statements of competencies expected of individuals, but instead upon the production of generalized statements on the educational background of members of the profession.[3]

As to accreditation, since 1957 the ALA accredits only the entry level professional programs at the master's level and the process—purely voluntary—has no legal sanction. Certification, the recognition by an agency of an individual who meets predetermined qualifications, typically may include completion of a set amount of work experience. Mahmoodi identifies only two library associations which perform certification in the library field: the American Association of Law Libraries uses academic background and/or work experience, while the Medical Library Association uses academic background and competency based testing of performance. School librarians are certified in all fifty states, usually by State Boards of Education. Public librarians certification is on the state level and is not standardized. Standards tend to be guidance for library service, not of competencies of those offering the service.[4] Mahmoodi concludes that statements on competencies point to a specialized body of knowledge broadly defined, usually acquired through special training. The few organizational attempts to identify competencies, according to Mahmoodi, tend to be on amounts of training and experience needed for a position.[5]

More recently when consulted, the RASD staff identified one recent organizational attempt to list competencies. The Young Adult Services Division (YASD) of ALA developed "a list of competencies which librarians working with young adults in any type of information agency should be able to demonstrate." The list was developed by a committee in 1981 and is published in the September 1982 issue of *School Library Journal.*[6] Seven areas are noted:

1. leadership and professionalism (i.e., attitude and commitment),
2. knowledge of client group,
3. communication,
4. administration—planning and managing,
5. knowledge of materials,
6. access to information, and
7. services.

Six specifics are noted under "services" including such abilities as utilizing techniques, providing information services (including crisis intervention counseling along with online databases), instructing young adults, encouraging use, etc.

Furthermore, most enumerations of qualifications have been based on informed opinion rather than systematic research. Two exceptions to this last summary are Mahmoodi's study and an earlier one conducted by Anna Hall entitled "Selected Educational Objectives for Public Services Librarians: A Taxonomic Approach."[7] Mahmoodi's study uses a goal-analysis procedure whereby the burden of identifying required competencies for public services jobs rests with incumbents. Hall's study attempted to identify "abilities" also by surveying public services librarians and then comparing these to five library school curriculums. Based on her 1968 research, Hall concludes that subjects important to public services generally are not taught and those that are taught are presented at an awareness level only. Courses aimed to develop higher skills were usually electives and thus were missed by most students. Finally she notes that instruction stresses factual knowledge, neglecting the complex intellectual skills required.[8]

Mahmoodi's survey conducted in 1976 among Minnesota public libraries identified fifty-three competencies, grouped in five categories: (1) the ability to identify individual and community information needs; (2) the ability to select, package and provide information; (3) the ability to evaluate services; (4) the ability to manage services; and (5) the ability to have general skills and attitudes conducive to provide public services activities.[9] Interestingly, Mahmoodi found that:

> in responding to the questionnaire individually, they rejected one skill—ability to conduct effective searches of machine-readable data bases—as of no importance (not needed) for current practice. They accepted all competencies as of at least some importance for ideal practice.[10]

Hall however, as Mahmoodi notes, identified a related competency, "to know which are the tried and proven applications of machines and equipment to the automation of specific library procedures as well as what new applications are presently being tested."[11] Mahmoodi concludes from the results of her research that, "competencies related to selection, organization' and dissemination of information, knowledge of the community, interpersonal communication and supervision are perceived as of great importance to current practice." Also attitudes are seen to be equally as important to public services librarianship as knowledge and skills.[12]

A historical review of reference services by Thomas Galvin appearing in the *Encyclopedia of Library and Information Science*[13] traces a few trends which contribute to today's concept of what reference librarians aim to do. Although reference is only one component of public services, it is perhaps the most representative and traditionally the most identified public services function.

As Galvin points out, historically the function of reference work during the nineteenth century included assisting students, developing the role of the library as an educational institution, helping the reader make the best reading selections, and justifying the library's existence by demonstrating its value to its funders.[14] The twentieth-century development added the growth of separate departments dedicated to reference services coupled with the emergence of subject divisions which decentralized the reference function and developed central "ready reference" service. The growth of the special library movement also greatly improved reference services in subject settings.[15] Galvin characterizes a minimal level of reference services held in common among all types of libraries today to include (1) assistance and instruction in library use, (2) assistance in the identification and selection of materials relevant to information needs, and (3) providing brief factual information (ready reference).[16] His list of activities which are offered in settings of amplified service may extend the traditional "reference services" role to that more all encompassing "public services." These activities include compiling literature searches, preparing user guides and selection aids, constructing special indexes, interlibrary loan, abstracting, translating, selective dissemination of information tailored to personal profiles, and editorial and publishing services.[17]

These activities share a few components which essentially characterize public services in libraries. Primarily, they involve personal interaction with the user, initially to gain input on his information need and subsequently, and to varied degrees, to deliver the information, to obtain feedback, and on occasion to promote the library resources through instruction or marketing. Second, the common component involves the intellectual process of translating the user's statement of need to the framework of the resources which may store the desired information. Third, a resource is somehow selected, examined and information sought in it, effectively done only if the resource is well understood. Finally, a tradition of most public services is to assist the user toward becoming self-sufficient in acquiring information, and thus librarians tend to share their knowledge of how to do it. To accomplish these activities, the abilities required (as noted earlier) are those to communicate, to analyze, to retrieve, and to instruct.

Let us briefly identify specific skills falling into each of the five proposed categories of competencies. First is the ability to communicate. It is most frequently demonstrated in the public services setting by the successful completion of an exchange with the user known as the "reference interview." Here the basic skills to master include the capability to effectively listen, to show empathy, to project verbally and nonverbally an approachability, and the ability to confidently articulate the options available to the user at various stages of his search for information. Reference interviewing is sometimes characterized to be an art, requiring an innate personality more than a learnable set of skills. An open, caring, inquisitive, approachable personality may favorably affect the interaction, but many of the required communication skills can be acquired. Another situation in which the librarian's communication abilities are seen is marketing. To complement the interpersonal communication skills, marketing techniques require abilities from the promoter; the abilities to understand the audience well enough to present the promoted product or service in relevant terms. To "sell" the concept or specific services of a library today is an extension of what Galvin described as a key function of nineteenth-century librarianship—to justify to funders. These skills are not widespread expectations of librarians, but are more frequently emerging as the competition for survival in the information marketplace increases.

The second category of competency suggested includes the ability to analyze information need. This process occurs both on an individual level and on a community level. Analysis of need is a key element necessary to link users with sources of needed information. The process, as any reference librarian knows, entails encoding the user's request to the search parameters of the system organizing the stored information. This encoding is an intellectual process involving an analysis of the request into related conceptual groups which each can be identified by terms comparable with the index vocabulary of the resource. For example, identifying a book on a given subject requires a translation of the subject into headings used in the card catalog searched. Sometimes knowledge of various languages is needed.

On a larger scale, public services librarians' analysis of the community's needs contributes to the design of library services offered and collections developed. Skills needed to effectively perform such analysis include evaluation, survey and statistical techniques. Again communication skills—both interpersonal and mass—become a necessary ability to master.

Such research activities, whether performed intuitively, informally or systematically, must be conducted to maintain an effective means to set service objectives.

The third category proposed to be essential for public services librarians is the ability to retrieve needed data. Skills required to perform this essential service include a contextual knowledge of sources and an awareness of the mechanics of utilizing them. Subject background becomes essential in some specialized situations, especially as user contact is decentralized into settings of subject orientation such as in special or branch libraries. The intellectual organization of the resource's information should be understood. The mechanics of using specific tools must also be mastered to effectively retrieve information. Various citation indexing methods, cataloging rules and filing rules, for example, govern the organization of much bibliographic data and demand a working familiarity to use them.

Instruction, the fourth category, may be an extension of communication skills, but because its objective is different, it has been identified separately here. One traditional role of the library has been to be an educational institution accomplished not only through knowledge gained by reading its stored information, but also by supplying methods of acquiring that information. The recent interest in library instruction, especially in the academic library setting, is an extension of this traditional function. Skills required are those of effective teaching and of developing user aids such as pathfinders and other bibliographic listings.

Finally, though not unique to public services librarians, most professionals need to be able to manage operations and supervise staff. The public services librarians participating in Mahmoodi's study estimated that 25 percent of their time was devoted to supervisory and administrative activities. Effective planning, budgeting, training, and personnel handling require learning managerial skills. Personality characteristics such as leadership, creativity and energetic dynamism contribute to effective administration.

These five categories will be the points of reference in this paper as we consider the impact of technology on public services librarians' competencies. They each may have variations in application to different library settings, to different users' services or community size; however, they are basic to all public services activities.

Impact of Technologies on Public Services

The technologies most prevalent in public services sections of libraries are seen in automated information retrieval systems, including databases of indexes, online card catalogs and machine-readable reference sources. Microcomputers are quickly adding user-friendly interfaces to larger systems, personalized organization of data, management aids, localized computer-assisted instruction packages, and word processed lists for users. These applications of automation in libraries most directly have affected reference, circulation, interlibrary loan, and collection management. Audiovisual technology has also influenced public services with increased formats of storage such as microforms, cassettes, records, videotapes, and software. Media centers for educational and popular reading have quickly developed to service these new formats and library public relations offices utilize media and production to reach remote users. Advances in telecommunications, including data transmission networks, satellite and microwave communication systems, provide public services librarians and users quicker transfer of information for such activities as interlibrary loan, circulation, information retrieval, and document delivery.

Although the full impact of all these technologies may have varied effects on public services librarians, the emphasis here will focus on automation. Specifically the major changes in public services settings within the past decade have occurred in the growth of availability of online database services and computerized bibliographic utilities.

Online databases of bibliographic citations began to develop in the mid-1960s, many from government contracts to design methods to organize and retrieve scientific and technical literature. Publishers began to utilize machine-readable data storage techniques to create photocompositions for printing abstract and index tools. With developed software, these files could then be used to retrieve citations for tailor-made bibliographies. Online retrieval systems, each providing access to numerous databases through a vendor, became commercially available in the early 1970s. Today hundreds of bibliographic files and millions of records, as well as several numeric databases, are available in the information market. The major vendors, DIALOG, SDC and BRS, as well as numerous smaller vendors and producers, market their systems to all types of libraries. Using them, public services librarians can offer users quick and comprehensive retrieval, providing retrospective searches, ready reference, bibliographic verifications, state-of-the-art bibliographies and selective dissemination of information (SDI) updates to specific profiles.

Effect of Online Technologies on Librarians' Competencies

Several articles in the literature address the issue of skills required of online database searchers. Most of the skills identified fall into one of the categories of competencies described earlier as a requisite of public services librarians.

The first primary competency identified for public services librarians is the ability to communicate. The process of determining the user's need requires effective interview techniques whether the subsequent search for information is computer assisted or not. Somerville, in her 1982 *Database* article on the "Pre-search Reference Interview," identifies "person-to-person communication skills..." to be "among the most critical for conducting the effective interview."[18] The process requires attentive listening, encouraging questioning, empathy, and an established rapport. Mignon presented a paper during the 1978 ASIS Annual Meeting in which he reports the findings of a meeting of library educators who identified a set of key issues related to the training and qualifications of information professionals specializing in online searching. Among the standards for qualifying beginning searchers are "skills associated with user interviewing."[19] Van Camp, in her 1979 *Online* article describing the "Effective Search Analysts," identifies "people oriented" attributes, suggesting that "skills in communication and interpersonal relations are essential for successful question negotiation with the end-users and for enthusiastic promotion and marketing of the search service."[20] She further stresses the importance of projected empathy, open-ended questioning, awareness of nonverbal behavior, and establishing rapport with the user. As Somerville points out, these interpersonal communication and negotiation skills "are the same as for all reference interviews. Without effective people skills, it would be highly unlikely that one would identify the needed information."[21]

Similarly, the second category of competencies repeatedly identified as required of online searchers is the ability to analyze the information need. In an excellent 1979 article in *Online*, Dolan and Kremin address the factors to provide "quality control of search analysts." A combination of traits are described and include concept analysis, flexibility of thinking, ability to think in synonyms, anticipation of variant word forms and spellings, and self-confidence.[22] All are essential for the search analyst to analyze the user's statement of need and translate it to parameters compatible with the source of information. Van Camp stresses that the "ability to think in a logical and analytical manner is an absolute *must* to be effective in searching," and that the searcher should be skilled at problem solving, decision making, and organizing and accomplishing a number of tasks simultaneously.[23] Somerville also emphasizes conceptual skills, analytical skills, and the ability to think logically among attributes for successful search analysis. Thus, as with traditional information retrieval done by public services librarians, computer-assisted reference services require from the searcher an ability to conceptualize in order to formulate search strategies.

The third category of competencies identified earlier include skills needed to actually retrieve information from sources of recorded data.

Mignon describes this skill among the standards identified to qualify beginning searchers as having "a command of the heuristics of literature searching," and being able to map the information request into the database vocabulary and to modify the strategy online.[24] Somerville echoes these traits in her list which includes knowledge of file organization, understanding of indexing policies and vocabulary control, and knowledge of sources and subject.[25] Van Camp identifies a few other skills necessary for effective searchers, including "knowledge of the subject areas in which the bulk of searching is to be done..." perseverance, patience, and efficient, organized work habits.[26] Again, as with manual searching, online retrieval requires the understanding of the content and organization of the sources of information as well as the access language and mechanics. Hammer suggests that familiarity with printed reference resources and reference experience are key sources for developing these required skills.[27]

User instruction skills compose the fourth category of competencies identified earlier. Dreifuss investigates "Library Instruction in the Database Searching Context" in his 1982 article in *RQ*. He argues that the five chartacteristics essential to any successful library instruction program exist in both traditional and online settings and advocates integrating instruction and computer-assisted searching services. These components include student motivation, timeliness of presentation, faculty support, and concept-oriented instruction.[28] The public services librarian needs efficient teaching techniques as well as planning and organization of materials. In providing traditional library instruction, librarians aim to facilitate the user's abilities to be self-sufficient in satisfying his/her information needs. At present, most user instruction about online services offered by librarians aims to inform the user about the sources, but not how to use them directly. The user remains dependent on the librarian intermediary. Some investigation is underway to create more "user-friendly" access systems to wean users from this dependency, but prototypes are not yet widely available. Greater progress is being made in the area of user-friendly access systems in the growing development of online catalogs. Various system designs and microcomputer interface programs are appearing in libraries to eliminate the end user's need for an intermediary to provide access to machine-stored information.

Instruction skills for online searching, however, are frequently required for in-house staff training. Vendors, database producers, associations, and consultants offer a wide variety of training sessions but most charge a substantial fee. Typically, many librarians utilize in-house training to expand staff skills and responsibility, for such education frequently rests with an online searcher. Van Camp includes the ability to share knowledge with others as one essential quality for effective search analysts.[29]

Several competencies not unique to public services librarians are identified in the literature as qualifications for online searching and should be mentioned to complete the discussion of expected skills. Again, they are equally important for the successful performance of traditional public services. Self-confidence is identified as a necessary characteristic to facilitate decision-making (by Dolan and Kremin), to reflect commitment to the professional activity of information retrieval and to eliminate any potential intimidation by computers (Van Camp). An attitude of commitment and inquiry is also vital to successful searching.

Test on Current Job Descriptions

Most of the views expressed thus far are based on personal observation and the informed opinion of other searchers expressing themselves in the literature. Additional research, similar to Mahmoodi and Hall's earlier studies, is needed to provide more substantial data on what skills public services librarians need to continue to provide user services as technology affects our ability to do so. In particular, I was curious to see how some of these observations about required competencies are reflected in practice. Without any pretense to following scientific methodology, I examined a sample of the fifty job announcements for vacant public services positions listed in the most recent two issues (March and April 1983) of *American Libraries*.

Responsibilities listed to qualify as a public services position included reference services, online searching, bibliographic instruction, circulation, interlibrary loan, and the management or administration of these activities. In addition, some listings for these assignments also included responsibility for collection development or selection of materials, public relations, liaison with user groups, and technical processing tasks. Nearly half (22) of the positions specifically cite responsibilities for performing computer-assisted services, mostly database searching (18), but also managing online circulation systems (4). The thirty-one academic library positions listed were nearly evenly split between those involving responsibilities with automated systems (16) and without (15); the fifteen public library positions, however, involved fewer assignments with automated services (5) than without (10). Special (3) and school (1) library positions listings were too few to analyze this way.

Among the twenty-two positions listing responsibilities for automated services, six specified no qualifications involving computer skills, and sixteen listed such competencies for applicants (eight each as requirements or as desired or preferred qualifications). Interestingly, of the remaining twenty-eight positions which specifically did not list any automated services responsibilities, nearly one-third (10) cited competencies in automated activities in the expected qualifications, four as requirements and six as desirable of applicants; eighteen noted no expectations of such skills.

Competencies involving automated activities were most frequently listed as "experience with online systems" (12) or "familiarity" or knowledge of online systems (11); occasionally (6) training or acquired skills were expected. Several other qualifications, not related to technology, were more frequently listed in these sampled job vacancies. These include an M.L.S. degree (44), additional subject-related education (30), experience in specific tasks (25), general library experience (20), ability to communicate (17), and managerial experience (15). Other qualifications listed include knowledge of collection development or resources (10); personality factors such as innovativeness, leadership, energy and dynamism (9); knowledge of foreign languages (5); service attitudes (5); and demonstrated research abilities (3). One might speculate from this small sample that libraries tend to primarily value experience, education and the ability to communicate when selecting public services librarians. Experience or familiarity with automated systems qualifies applicants about as frequently as knowledge of other sources and personality traits conducive to public services. The lack of more specific mention of qualities such as analytical methods or retrieval techniques might be a result of our profession not yet having clear measures of such competencies. Library educators and practitioners are both challenged to better understand the role of these traits in designing the training and methods of qualifying attainment of these competencies.

Look at the Future

As stated at the outset, the perspective of this paper has been strictly past and present. Viewed in terms of today's requirements, public services librarians basically must have the same competencies to use automated technology as did the previous generation who did not face computerization. Communication skills remain paramount. Analytical abilities, knowledge of retrieval systems and sources, and instruction techniques are necessary to perform effective public services and perhaps have become more explicitly required with the appearance of automated services. Experience and education continue to be the primary measure of attaining required competencies.

There seems to be an implied higher expectation of librarians to provide precise, accurate information with the use of online systems than was previously experienced. The costs—calculated with each instance of use of automated resources—and the visibility of errors—such as incorrect logic, improper selection of files or terms, and misspelling—both contribute to a rising sense of accountability among public services librarians using online sources. These same factors, however, hidden in the costs of staff time and users' convenience, existed before in traditional public services. The experiences of providing online services and the resulting sensitivity to efficiency, user satisfaction and cost effectiveness should be actively applied to other public services and should aggressively contribute to development of library service philosophies. Aside from relatively minor adjustments in mastering new techniques and understanding new resources, the impact of technology today on public services librarians falls within this area of perfecting existing competencies.

But the situation may or may not change in the future. To consider future trends, the remainder of this paper can only be based on speculation. Lancaster provides a very plausible forecast of the future of publishing and the corresponding changing role of librarians in an upcoming paperless society. In an article by Lancaster, Drasgow and Marks, current trends are projected to offer a scenario of what the role of libraries may be by the end of the century. The prediction includes "a rapid decline of the artifact— particularly the printed book..." and an "increasing diversification in the profession..." where information specialists will not need to function from a library.[30] Publishing will continue to rely more on electronic means, until eventually information will be accessible primarily in machine-readable form. Electrobooks, online journals, electronic mail, and computer conferencing exist today, and, as Lancaster argues, will likely replace present methods of information recording and distribution. In turn, access to sources of information will be made most often from individuals' homes and offices and will not require going to a separate library facility. Most individuals in all fields will conduct their own searches.

"Considerable trauma" is predicted to occur within the profession during the transition to the electronic library. We have already begun to witness anxiety about the future role of librarians, their replacement by machines and the obsolescence of print tools. Lancaster predicts the "dwindling away of technical services in general...a very considerable reduction in interlibrary loan traffic," the reduction of staff, and the remaining library activities to be highly service oriented.[31] Lancaster suggests a new dichotomy may occur between those librarians handling electronic information sources and those concerned with print and microform tools, as well as one between generalists in libraries and subject specialists not necessarily affiliated with libraries who work more closely with research teams in the capacity of retrieving information. Librarians become information consultants, linking users with data in subject areas with which they may be less familiar—e.g., in the academic library setting. Public librarians will facilitate terminal access for those who may wish to retrieve information from the library and will assist users with general and difficult question-answering services. School librarians will provide access to computer-assisted instruction facilities and recreational materials. As costs of storage, retrieval and communication continue to diminish, the gap between the information rich and the information poor should be reduced.[32]

Lancaster's persuasive predictions about the future role and requirements of librarians in the next twenty years or so extends the need for many of the competencies identified in this paper, but suggests that the setting of their utilization will change. The major change is that although the term *librarian* may remain associated with those professionals performing archival-like work affiliated with libraries, the new public servant is an "information consultant" or "information specialist" not requiring the physical facilities of a library. The needs in the electronic age will be for "a detailed knowledge of electronic information resources together with the terminals and expertise needed to exploit these resources effectively." Similar to their library counterparts, these information consultants help "to put those with information needs in touch with data bases or individuals likely to be able to satisfy these needs." Furthermore, they will provide a more complete range of sources and the delivery of information.[33]

Educational objectives of these future professionals suggest the expected competencies to be needed. According to Lancaster, knowledge of the communication process, of publication and dissemination processes, of interpersonal communication, of design and management of information services, of evaluation methods, and of how to retrieve data and exploit resources will need to be part of the curriculum.[34] Thorough familiarity with communication activities, such as electronic mail systems, computer conferencing, communication networks and word processing, and text editing systems and equipment are required. Some future librarians will be responsible for the electronic organization of internal company files and sources of information dissemination which places them in a critical position to influence the design and usability of online resources potentially to be used by others.

The seldom stated requirement of anyone in a public access position is that of flexibility and common sense. The implied characteristic of a professional is inquisitiveness and continued self-education. Together these qualities will facilitate today's public services librarians to adjust their existing competencies in the areas of communication, analysis, retrieval, and instruction to meet the challenges offered by new sources of information and the techniques to utilize them in the electronic future.

REFERENCES

1. Hammer, Mary M. "Search Analysts as Successful Reference Librarians." *Behavioral & Social Sciences Librarian* 2(Winter 1981/Spring 1982):222.
2. Mahmoodi, Suzanne Hoegh. "Identification of Competencies for Librarians Performing Public Services Functions in Public Libraries." Ph.D. diss., University of Minnesota, 1978, p. 11.
3. Ibid., pp. 2-3.
4. Ibid., p. 22.
5. Ibid., p. 42.
6. American Library Association. Young Adult Services Division. Education Committee. "Young Adults Deserve the Best: Competencies for Librarians Saving Youth." *School Library Journal* 29(Sept. 1982):51.
7. Hall, Anna. "Selected Educational Objectives for Public Services Librarians: A Taxonomic Approach." Ph.D. diss., University of Pittsburgh, 1968. (During discussions following the presentation of this paper another sutdy was brought to the author's attention. See Baxter, Barbara Ann. "History and Analysis of a Competency-Based Certification Examination for Health Sciences Librarians." Master's thesis, University of Chicago Graduate Library School, 1982. Readers may be especially interested in chapters 1 and 2 which provide a detailed and thorough historical and bibliographical review of the topic.)
8. Ibid., pp. 152-53.
9. Mahmoodi, "Identification of Competencies," pp. 74-75.
10. Ibid., p.109.
11. Ibid., p. 10.
12. Ibid., p. 11.
13. Galvin, Thomas J. "Reference Services and Libraries." In *Encyclopedia of Library and Information Science*, vol. 25, edited by Allen Kent, et al., pp. 210-26. New York: Marcel Dekker, 1978.
14. Ibid., p. 213.
15. Ibid., p. 214.
16. Ibid., p. 220.
17. Ibid., p. 221.
18. Somerville, Arleen N. "The Pre-Search Reference Interview—A Step by Step Guide." *Database* 5(Feb. 1982):32.
19. Mignon, Edmond. "Emerging Perspectives on the Teaching of Online Searching As a Professional Specialization." In *The Information Age in Perspective* (Proceedings of the ASIS Annual Meeting), vol. 15, compiled by Everett H. Brenner, p. 227. White Plains, N.Y.: Knowledge Industry Publications, 1978.
20. Van Camp, Ann. "Effective Search Analysts." *Online* 3(April 1979):18-19.
21. Somerville, "The Pre-Search Reference Interview," p. 34.
22. Dolan, Donna R., and Kremin, Michael. "The Quality Control of Search Analysts." *Online* 3(April 1979):9.
23. Van Camp, "Effective Search Analysts," p. 18.
24. Mignon, "Emerging Perspectives on the Teaching of Online Searching," pp. 226-27.
25. Somerville, "The Pre-Search Reference Interview," p. 32.
26. Van Camp, "Effective Search Analysts," pp. 19-20.
27. Hammer, "Search Analysts as Successful Reference Librarians," p. 23.
28. Dreifuss, Richard A. "Library Instruction in the Database Searching Context." *RQ* 21(Spring 1982):234-36.
29. Van Camp, "Effective Search Analysts," p. 20.
30. Lancaster, F. Wilfrid, et al., "The Changing Face of the Library: A Look at Libraries and Librarians in the Year 2001." *Collection Management* 3(Spring 1979):56.
31. Ibid., pp. 68-69.
32. Ibid., pp. 70-71.
33. Ibid., pp. 73-74.
34. Ibid., p.75.

RICHARD T. SWEENEY
Executive Director
Public Library of Columbus and Franklin County
Columbus, Ohio

The Public Librarian of the Last Years of the Twentieth Century

This paper addresses two major questions. First, what is the schizophrenia that is afflicting the library profession in general and public librarians in particular? Second, what knowledge and skill competencies must public librarians possess to survive in the remainder of this century, particularly in utilizing information technology? In the latter part of this paper I will suggest six competency areas that should be emphasized both for public librarians and all professional librarians.

Most public librarians have difficulty thinking of libraries as just one type of information technology. The general public thinks of public libraries primarily as a collection of books or a room or building where a collection of books, periodicals, manuscripts, or even possibly video-cassettes are kept. Clearly, to meet their needs, people go to many other information resources than just the public library. Today, the emergence of videotex, teletex, autodial tape services, electronic banking services, electronic publishing, laser printing on demand, and many other technologies are expanding the information user's options.

My home copy of the *World Book Dictionary* defines librarian as: "1. a person in charge of a library or part of a library, 2. a person trained for work in a library...."[1] Compare this definition of a librarian with the definition for a physician in the same book: "1. a doctor of medicine,... 2. any practitioner of the healing art...."[2] Using the same criteria to describe librarians as were used for physicians, I arrived at the following definition; a librarian is "1. a doctor of knowledge, 2. any practitioner of the art of satisfying information quests." This should demonstrate the schizophrenia that splits our profession—public librarianship especially. The popular notion of librarians as people in charge of libraries is being challenged by the trends of the new technology and the philosophical basis for librarianship. Physicians are not defined by their work in hospitals. They are defined by the activity or service they provide to people—i.e., healing.

Librarians should not and must not be defined by a place—i.e., a library or even by a type of media such as the book. They should not be defined by print, audiovisual materials or computers either. Librarians should *use* various technologies but not be defined by any. Technology is the means—not the end. Librarians must be defined by their service or activity for people.

In the popular and extensively quoted *Megatrends,* John Naisbitt says: "If you don't know what business you are in, conceptualize what business it would be useful for you to think you are in."[3] If the telephone company can claim to be in the knowledge business, as their ads proclaim, then surely librarians can redefine their business likewise. This is not just a case of semantics but rather a case of understanding roles and consequently the competencies and skills that librarians must possess.

Lancaster in his new book, *Libraries and Librarians In An Age Of Electronics,*[4] speaks of the new librarian as one not tied to libraries bound by walls. The technology now makes possible the remote electronic delivery of information so that patrons and librarians will not be bound by buildings as they have been. However, the notion of the librarians as caretakers of buildings and collections has been ingrained for hundreds of years, and is a cornerstone of traditional concepts of librarianship. This author, for one, would hope that the profession recognizes this split and begin to bring the parts together in a logical evolution.

There have been three major inventions or developments that have given birth to, and subsequently revolutionized, librarianship. The first was the invention of writing which enabled the recording of information leading to the storage, organization and dissemination services of the first libraries. This lasted for a few thousand years. The second invention was that of the printing press which provided rapid, inexpensive replications of original works and made possible the "popular libraries," or public libraries as we know them. The printing press has been around for only approximately 500 years. The first invention (writing) made libraries possible, and the second (the printing press) made them available to most people.

The third invention is the marriage of computers and telecommunications into videotex and information systems designed for home/office self service by the average person. Since this is such a new development, some may argue that it is premature to put it into the same category as the printing press or the invention of writing in its effects upon libraries. However, videotex information services can be made available wherever people are, whenever they want them and provide a volume of information the world's greatest libraries cannot meet. This new development, which is only now beginning, will radically change the future of the library profession.

The electronic library, as I prefer to call it, is characterized by patrons searching for the information they need directly on computer terminals remote from the database. While the electronic library is meant to be a more independent service, the complexity of searching large numbers of databases of complete text linked together in intricate networks will require remote searching assistance. The concept of librarians providing assistance to patrons, some of whom are in a distant location, while "walking" them through a search is a promising continuation of the best part of our profession.

The new developments with information technology are viewed as an aberration by traditional librarians who believe the library is primarily a collection of books and have accepted only sparingly other documents and packages such as phonodiscs, films, videocassettes, and even computer programs. The remote electronic delivery of information is not their notion of the role of the librarian. On the other hand, there are the library technocrats who believe libraries should be shaped and administered by the computer specialists, the programmers, the telecommunication experts, indeed, all of the technologists. They believe that the book should be replaced as outmoded.

Information technology is too important to be left to technologists. The professionals who are charged with the responsibility for meeting and satisfying the information requests of the public must manage the information technology themselves or be replaced by it. Librarians must learn to manage information technology and this requires first some attitudinal changes.

A recent study completed by the large management-consulting company, Booz, Allen and Hamilton, Inc., and reviewed in *Business Week* magazine, states "about a third of all 'knowledge workers'—a catchall term that includes professionals and executives—will be wary of the computer terminal rather than receptive to it."[5] About one out of ten managers have such fear and mistrust of the new technology that they are unlikely to deal with it first hand. While age will affect the managers' attitudes, tenure with a single organization for over twenty-five years is likely to result in a resister. Ironically, educational level does not appear to be a significant factor. The study indicates that the manager's attitude toward the typewriter and skill at using it appear to predict her/his success at approaching the terminal keyboard.

I have heard it said that there are three things in life which are unavoidable, not two. These are death, taxes and change. The library profession, I believe, has more than its share of resisters whose basic attitudes are shaped by fear and who resist change. The first basic chore of the library profession with respect to librarians and information technology is to redirect the fear—the attitudes of the resisters—so that librarians will become more productive managers and users of information technology. Furthermore, the new candidates studying to be librarians must be screened so that they possess a positive constructive attitude toward technology. This means understanding that information technology is here to stay, that it must be effectively utilized by librarians and that it cannot do everything.

This paper proposes six new competency areas for public librarians given the new information technology. All six of these involve a greater sphere of knowledge while only two involve a direct skill. Naisbitt in *Megatrends* says: "In an information economy, then, value is increased not by labor, but by knowledge...."[6]

The six new competencies are not new, nor are they exhaustive. I have deliberately avoided some important skills that are now being addressed in many graduate library programs and will soon be in others, such as searching remote machine-readable databases, search strategy, networking, and information theory. Such knowledge and skills are vitally important to librarians today, and are generally recognized as such.

This paper also deliberately avoids computer programming, science, systems analysis, mathematics, and statistics, the study of which should be prerequisites for admission into graduate library programs. They are crucial to the fundamentally broad background of the professional librarian, but should not be placed on the graduate level.

The first appointment that I made to the data processing department in our public library was a librarian. None of the others had even a bachelor's degree much less a professional library degree. The appointment of a librarian without a technical background who had been a branch head was looked upon by some inside and outside of the library as a waste of money if not an actual hindrance. The broad liberal arts background, the public service orientation, and the ability to see the bigger picture have proven invaluable. Programmers and computer operators need a strong technical background, but systems designers, planners and decision makers need a strong professional library orientation. Our data processing manager, while not a professional librarian, worked his way up the library ranks, having been both a page and a bookmoblie driver. Fortunately he is not only technically competent, but also library experienced.

The philosophy that a data processing manager of a public library must be a technically experienced data processing professional has to be weighed against the likelihood of rapid turnover and the lack of a passionate love or understanding of libraries or librarians in the person who makes the decisions and sets the priorities in the technical area.

In February, I had the privilege of speaking to some of the faculty and students at Ohio University regarding the electronic library and the effects of the information technology on society in general. On the program with me was Charles Hildreth, a research scientist doing excellent work at OCLC. It was only after we were both introduced that I realized that we each had liberal arts backgrounds and yet were speaking on the new information technology as "experts."

The ability to understand and communicate with librarians, users and the technology experts is not likely to be found with data processing "bits and bytes" people. Give me a liberal arts trained librarian who is willing and eager to learn over an engineer or computer scientist who is willing to "understand" librarians. The future, ironically, belongs to the generalist, not the specialist.

The first new competency needed, therefore, by public librarians is managing information technology. The public library profession needs visionary people who understand, can utilize and manage information technology. They must understand and know both the limits of the technology as well as the potential. Unfortunately most librarians have had only one course in administration and management and one in library automation, yet they are not educated in managing new technology. This has left many public library administrators at the mercy of library automation vendors, well meaning but biased consultants, or technical staff who talk in "j buffer terminology." Many library administrators are forced to learn the equivalent of quantum physics without any formal training, without a textbook and in quick conversations with overworked staff. It is the school of experience where one wrong decision is magnified, in some cases, to millions of dollars, and costs careers. This lack of knowledge on how to manage the new technology is not theoretically sound or practically tolerable.

Well-educated and experienced library administrators are just as vulnerable as their less experienced colleagues because the new technology is managed differently in some areas from traditional library resources. For example, an excellent article in *Business Week* last year on managing technology said: "One thing is certain: Assumptions grounded in evolutionary, incremental thinking will be severely tested."[7]

Technologies can be either evolutionary or revolutionary. That is, some technologies can evolve from others while some are revolutionary and replace the old completely. The article goes on to say about alpha sites.

> The record is uncomfortably clear. Technology leaders tend to become technology losers. A few companies manage transitions to new technological fields effectively, but many others are unable even to begin the process, and most find it impossible to complete the move successfully.[8]

Even fewer public libraries will find it possible to manage the transition to the electronic library. While the lack of research and development, and the lack of investment capital and political inertia are very important obstacles, the most serious is the lack of skilled information technology managers. An information technology manager knows the technical limits of a new technology, the unrealized potential of technology, the proper time and method for migrating from a mature technology without withdrawing too quickly so as to lose user support. He knows the risks inherent in making transitions, and finally, the often greater risks of avoiding the transitions.

Library directors and managers tend to assume that change will occur at approximately the same rate of speed as in the past and that the rate can be controlled. This is an unfortunate assumption that has failed consistently. Consider that library directors do not typically change their information tehnology goals, directions and speed, but rather boards of trustees change their library directors.

Library patrons cannot be relied upon to decide what might be possible from the new technology. It must be initiated by the professionals. Five or ten years ago who would have guessed the need for something like Donkey Kong, Centipede or Pac Man? There is an article that appeared in a 1982 issue of the *Harvard Business Review* on computerized manufacturing, which says some things that are applicable to libraries:

> This leap in complexity [that is, computers] also prompts some companies to rely too heavily on vendors to solve problems....Turnkey projects, in which vendors assume all responsibility for making the system work are particularly dangerous. Building up in-house experience is critical.... Begin to worry the very moment your...people tell you with reference to some problem or other, "Don't worry, that's the vendor's responsibility."[9]

We cannot shirk the responsibility of understanding, planning and managing the technology or we will have reason to worry.

The first new major skill or competency area that all public professional librarians must possess then consists of the principles of managing information technology and would be a likely requisite in all graduate librarian programs. Planning is a way of life for professionals. The second new major competency area is keeping informed about the *state of the art of specific information technologies*. Every librarian must understand the current application of nonlibrary, as well as library, information technologies that are available in the marketplace.

Typically we learn in library school about automated circulation systems and perhaps bibliographic utilities. Unfortunately this presentation is often not only cursory but out of date. If we are fortunate, we have learned the advantages and disadvantages of some of these and a framework for selecting the efficient and effective. Perhaps we learned the RFP (Request for Proposal) process. Unfortunately this knowledge has been seriously inadequate and does not reflect the real world.

It is as important that every librarian know the state-of-the-art of electronic banking and publishing as it is to know about current online public access catalogs. Most of the nonlibrary information technology is not reviewed in the standard library literature or in most graduate programs, and yet this technology is likely to bring some of the most innovative and efficient future applications to libraries. There is a large difference between typical library automation course work and the range and depth of understanding of specific technologies.

A third new area of professional librarian competency follows quickly after the second and might be called *the future, or developing, information technologies.* These would include technologies which are technically feasible today—although perhaps not yet economically feasible—as well as future research and development into information technology. For instance, this body of knowledge should include the areas of artificial intelligence, laser printing on demand, videotex, and new information storage possibilities such as optical laser discs. Such knowledge is necessary in planning for the future and deciding on the possible implications to the library profession's role.

Last summer, the conservative and widely read business magazine, *Fortune,* did an entire series on robots and artificial intelligence and their effect on the business environment. One of those articles, entitled "Computers On the Road to Self Improvement," made a statement regarding artificial intelligence that should make us think about our future:

> Ever since intelligent machines first began to be talked about, humans have assured themselves that no matter how proficient machines [computers] become at math..., chess, understanding plain English, or whatever, they would never be able to exhibit true creativity. Unfortunately for that premise, inventing electronic devices and heuristic ways of thinking, probably qualifies as creative by...any standard. So those who still seek to demonstrate the innate superiority of human beings will have to redraw the comfort lines elsewhere.[10]

Personally I do believe in the innate superiority of human beings but not simply for the reasons of intelligence and creativity which the author indicated. There is every reason to suspect that, with the developments of artificial intelligence, for example, the routine ready reference services of today will become mostly automated and self-service. There will be no need for a librarian to answer—for the fiftieth time today—the major vita of, for example, the Russian premier or the address of the local state senator. Librarians should play an important part in the design of such systems and in making them user friendly. How far such systems are in the future and what their implications are should be the concern of professional librarian think tanks at our graduate library and information programs which will keep the profession prepared for the most likely eventualities. But all librarians who consider themselves professionals must keep abreast of the new developments and measure these against their role: practicing the art of satisfying information quests.

A fourth area of competency is the *analysis and diagnostics of information-seeking behavior*. Understanding users and how they search for information is much broader than reference interrogation, although that represents a good start. It includes understanding patrons' needs which were not completely met or even those who never posed the question in the first place because they could not overcome emotional or other obstacles. How will users react when they search on self-service computer terminals, possibly in the privacy of their own homes? What happens when they need help? This might be considered the professional equivalent of the physician's bedside manner. It is important that library patrons feel personally comfortable and satisfied with sufficient and accurate information provided to them in a timely fashion.

A series of articles appeared last year in *Impact: Information Technology* published by the Administrative Management Society on the people issues of office automation. The article says: "The essense of the people-oriented approach may be summarized in one statement: people don't change unless they want to. If users don't support a project, it is unlikely to succeed."[11] If the electronic library is going to succeed it must take into consideration three factors noted in this article. Patrons must really want a system in order to willingly change their working patterns. Second, the greatest payoffs will come from systems directed at the problems that are key to the patron's success. Third the article says that only patrons (and librarians) are in a position to "design" systems (in their own terms) that are usable, functional and flexible.

We must better understand our patrons and their needs. We must be more client-oriented. The behavorial sciences are not as precise as mathematics, but the people issues are more important. Our users may be the most forgotten factor in typical library automation projects, but they certainly are the most important.

The fifth new competency that all public librarians must possess is *understanding the societal issues that develop from the information technology*. Everyone understands that librarians do not live—and should not live—in vacuums. Yet the average library professionals are not keeping themselves informed about and actively involved in, such changing issues as copyright, privacy, database security, the private sector *v.* the public sector information roles, the right of all citizens to a basic level of information regardless of their ability to pay, equality of access that is not geographically, politically or socially determined, and the freedom to intellectually pursue the information you want or need on an electronic system. There are questions of a more technical nature that will affect us also such as the common carrier status and franchising of the cable companies; the presentation level protocol standards of videotex that AT&T developed; the lack of standard, or even compatible, operating systems and software for computers; the problem of insufficient resolution of home television sets for graphic and textual information display; and so on. There are dozens of issues and standards that are being debated in Congress or by technical standard committees or other public forums that will have enormous effects upon us and most of us are silent and (much worse) ignorant about them.

The August 1982 edition of *Advanced Technology Libraries* reported that the Videotex '82 conference in New York was very large and well attended by information providers and videotex people from all over the world. It said: "Librarians...were nowhere to be found."[12]

These issues that have been discussed will need to be the subject of a great deal of research and development as well as open debate and discussion in the profession. There are too few resources in the profession to accomplish the agenda that needs to be met unless we focus on many of these critical items. This means that libraries will have to fund research and development projects out of their current budgets. How can we fund research, development and policy questions within already strained and inadequate library budgets? It's simple. Either we invest in our own future or we don't have any. The political reality is there facing us, pushing public libraries in the other direction toward perhaps our eventual demise as the information center of first resort in the community. The question is, can we afford not to defend and even attack the basic premise that we are a not-so-relevant institution any longer? I have lumped research and development with the concept of understanding the impact of the information technology on the societal issues because society will either accept or reject libraries in the future based on their development and usefulness.

John Naisbitt says: "We are drowning in information but starved for knowledge."[13] This is the basis for the last of the new competencies— *building knowledge bases*. It means that librarians must be involved in the process of organizing the electronic information delivery and access, providing a quality filtering and synthesis process that reduces much of the redundant and irrelevant information to just what a practitioner or scholar needs. The critical problem of the next twenty years is not having enough information but having only the necessary and relevant information that specifically meets the user's needs. An interesting initial step in this direction was taken at the National Library of Medicine on the development of a Hepatitis Knowledge Base.[14] It is designed to take from the thousands of articles published on that narrow field all the relevant information a practitioner needs and no more. It is an attempt to make the information overload problem manageable. While this process is in its infancy, its implication to all librarians is worth our attention.

The profession is schizophrenic due to the conflicting forces of the technocrats on the one hand and the traditional book librarians on the other. We must seek to maintain a balance, with our librarians being oriented toward the service of satisfying information quests regardless of the technology. We must also seek to add six new competencies to the body of skills and knowledge developed for our profession. These are (1) information technology management; (2) state-of-the-art specific information technologies; (3) the future, or developing information technologies; (4) analysis and diagnostics of information-seeking behavior; (5) understanding the societal issues that develop from the information technology; and (6) building knowledge bases. Every professional public librarian must be learning these new areas.

We have two views of the future of the public librarian that make a startling contrast to end this paper. They are two statements that give us a theoretical framework for our profession. The first view is by Carlton Rochell in last October's issue of *Library Journal*, who indicates that public libraries and librarians in the year 2000, "will lose a good many of their patrons to private sector information providers..." and they will "lose their business, and more important, will lose their financial and political support...."[15] The other is a quote about libraries by scientist Carl Sagan in *Cosmos*:

> The library connects us with the insights and knowledge, painfully extracted from Nature, of the greatest minds that ever were, with the best teachers, drawn from the entire planet and from all of our history, to instruct us without tiring, and to inspire us to make our own contribution to the collective knowledge of the human species....[16]

If public librarians adapt this noble philosophy to the changing technology and environment and constantly rethink and relearn new competencies, public libraries and librarians will flourish throughout the remainder of this century.

REFERENCES

1. *World Book Dictionary*, 6th ed., 1969, s.v. "librarian."
2. Ibid., s.v. "physician."
3. Naisbitt, John. *Megatrends: Ten New Directions Transforming Our Lives*. New York: Warner Books, 1982, p. 88.
4. Lancaster, F. Wilfrid. *Libraries and Librarians In An Age Of Electronics*. Arlington, Va.: Information Resources Press, 1982.

5. "How to Conquer Fear Of Computers." *Business Week* 29 March 1982, p. 176.

6. Naisbitt, *Megatrends*, p. 17.

7. "How To Conquer Fear Of Computers," p. 28.

8. Foster, Richard N. "A Call for Managing Technology." *Business Week* 24 May 1983.

9. Gerwin, Donald. "Dos and Don'ts of Computerized Manufacturing." *Harvard Business Review* 60(March/April 1982):115.

10. Alexander, Tom. "Computers On The Road to Self-Improvement." *Fortune* 105(14 June 1982):160.

11. Meyer, N. Dean. "The People Issues of Office Automation—Part 4." *Impact: Information Technology* 5(December 1982):2-4.

12. "Teletext to Debut On U.S. Networks." *Advanced Technology Libraries* 11(Aug. 1982):3.

13. Naisbitt, *Megatrends*, p. 24.

14. Bernstein, Lionel M., et al. "The Hepatitis Knowledge Base: A Prototype Information Transfer System." *Annals Of Internal Medicine* 93(July 1980):169-81, pt. 2.

15. Rochell, Carlton. "Telematics—2001 A.D." *Library Journal* 107(1 Oct. 1982):1814.

16. Sagan, Carl. *Cosmos*. New York: Random House, 1980, p. 282.

CAROLYN M. GRAY
Assistant Director
Technical Services and Automation
Brandeis University Library

Technology and the Academic Library Staff or the Resurgence of the Luddites

This clinic program announces that I intend to address the human factors involved in library automation in academic libraries. It is tempting to begin this talk by discussing the impact of technology upon academic library staff with a lead into the competencies that idea assumes. If I began in that way, I might begin with certain assumptions. Some of the assumptions held by many attending this conference might include:

1. that the application of technology in libraries will result in benefits to staff and users;
2. that technology is the inevitable wave of the future; and
3. that as librarians, if we do not embrace technology, we will be left to fade into oblivion in our museums full of books.

I prefer not to begin with those assumptions because I feel we have not fully explored the philosophical and ideological foundations of our views about the use of technology. The time available does not permit a full exploration of the philosophical and ideological foundations of our assumptions concerning technology. However time does give me an opportunity to pose some questions and to begin a dialogue among librarians concerning the human factors impacted by library technology. The beginning thesis of my discussion is drawn from a broader look at technology. It is my assertion that the ideological problems in technological applications in libraries result "from a fatalistic and futuristic confusion about the technological development, and this intellectual problem is rooted in, reinforced by, the political and ideological subordination of people"[1] in the work environment and at the point of service.

We are so enamored by the promises of the future applications and possibilities of technology that we lose sight of the human cataloger, serials clerk and the library patron. We promise increased control and a decrease in the rise of per unit costs of processing materials, but fail both to measure the human costs, and to assess the reality of the new application of technology.

I propose that we must take a multiple perspective approach to the analysis of human factors impacted by library technology. Any technological application in libraries must have the support of three distinct groups to achieve the greatest success:

1. the administration or funding agency must support the concepts initially so adequate funding can be secured;
2. the library staff responsible for implementing and using the system must be supportive or subtle, or not so subtle—sabotage may ensue; and
3. the users of the system must support the project in order to achieve acceptance and use after implementation.

These three perspectives may have contradictory needs: (1) the funding agency is concerned about initial and ongoing costs; (2) the library staff may be concerned about bibliographical integrity, MARC formats, and authority control; and (3) the users will want immediate access (no down time), simplicity of use and comprehensive coverage. These are some simple examples of needs identified in the multiple perspective approach to the analysis of the impact of technology. From these examples it is easy to see the variety of requirements and perceptions of need from the various groups. The problem which arises once one begins this analysis is that the perspectives are often contradictory. The funding considerations come into direct conflict with the need for comprehensive coverage.

The biggest reason for this apparent contradictory dilemma is that we do not look at the whole of the situation—a common systems analysis problem. Most systems' problems arise because we fail to think in broad enough terms. We look at the subsystem without considering the context. Physicist Niels Bohr, in another context, viewed apparent contradictions as being complementary in nature:

> In general philosophical perspective, it is significant that, as regards analysis and synthesis in other fields of knowledge, we are confronted with situations reminding us of the situation in quantum physics. Thus, the integrity of living organisms and the characteristics of conscious individuals and human cultures present features of wholeness, the account of which implies a typical complementary mode of description.[2]

The complementary nature of the three perspectives are a part of the whole systems approach to the analysis of the impact of technology.

Problems arise when the human factors are not considered. Michael Malinconico, writing in *Library Journal*, lists "the principal risks inherent in an attempt to introduce new technologies..." and "the factors which influence the potential level of risk..."[3] but nowhere does he mention staff or user acceptance as a potential risk or factor to be considered in avoiding failure. The entire article is devoted to the planning process, budget overruns, time delays, system failures, and the failure of the project to deliver on anticipated benefits. This is only one of many examples available in the literature where there is an ideological subordination of people in the discussion of system planning and implementation.

We are in danger of a resurgence of the Luddites if we do not fully acknowledge the importance of people in the successful planning and implementation of our grandiose plans for automating the library world. "Technology has been made to serve a cult of the 'future' such that the urgencies of the present are conveniently ignored."[4] A recent issue of *Democracy* looks at technology's politics in which private capital is accused of "moving decisively to enlarge and to consolidate the social dominance it secured in the first..." Industrial Revolution. "As their extortionist tactics daily diminish the wealth of nations, they announce anew the optimistic promises of technological deliverance and salvation through science." Those of us involved in the automation of libraries have been optimistically promising technological deliverance from drudgery, and are perpetuating the myth of technology "as an autonomous thing, beyond politics and society, with a destiny of its own....Technological determinism—the domination of the present by the future—have combined in our minds to annihilate the technological present. The loss of the concrete, the inevitable consequence of the subordination of people..." in the design and planning of automated systems "thus has resulted also in the loss of the present as the realm for assessments, decisions, and actions."[5] Noble further states that:

> The purpose here is to acknowledge, endorse, and encourage...[the library staff's] response to technology in the present tense, not in order to abandon the future but to make it possible. In politics it is always essential to construct a compelling vision of the future and to work toward it, and this is especially true with regard to technology. But it is equally essential to be able to act effectively in the present, to defend existing forces against assault and to try to extend their reach. In the absence of a strategy for the present, these forces will be destroyed and without them all talk about the future becomes merely academic.[6]

Social historians have attempted to reconstruct the trauma of the first Industrial Revolution and to look with new eyes at the Luddites—the machine smashers. The Luddites (we are told in the history of the Industrial Revolution) were opposed to progress—i.e., did not want their skilled weaving jobs replaced by giant mechanical looms. The Luddites went about smashing the machines to save their jobs in an attempt to buy time for themselves and adjust to the new technology. The Luddites were

reacting to technological progress in the present tense. Traditional historical accounts have been inherited from:

> those who opposed machinery breaking and who succeeded in removing
> the technology question from the point of production, from the workers
> themselves, from the present that was the first Industrial Revolution. In
> the place of that traumatic reality, they constructed technological myths
> about the power of the past and the promise of the future. And in the
> light of these myths the courageous Luddites were made to seem mis-
> taken, pathetic, dangerous and insane.[7]

When I speak of a resurgence of the Luddites, stories come to mind of
bibliographic sabotage by retrospective conversion staffs who entered
bogus, sometimes obscene records into the MARC format and entered them
into various systems. Without early involvement of the people affected by
the technological changes in the planning process, we set ourselves up for
failure. We are talking about more than minimal levels of competencies
needed to perform functions; we are talking about attitudes, resistance to
change and more.

When we involve in the planning process people to be affected by the
technological change, frank discussions should take place regarding staff
displacement. As administrators introducing new technologies into the
library environment we are all too quick to promise that, "no jobs will be
lost" as a result of automation. What we should be saying is that, "no
positions will be lost." We must introduce the idea of staff displacement in
light of new skills needed.

As the structure of the functions of reference, circulation, cataloging,
and acquisitions changes with the implementation of automated systems,
different skills are needed to perform in the new environment. Jobs change
radically and, though there may be no reduction in staff, there certainly is
displacement of staff. Staff who once worked somewhat autonomously
checking in journals in a public service area may find the job moved into
the technical services area because it is now possible to access the check-in
records from multiple locations via computer terminals.

We were formerly bound by the desire to give public access to a single
manual file of check-in records. The staff member who was in charge of
check-in and public assistance in use of the check-in file, now finds the job
totally split. When we look at that job we are not talking about FTEs
(full-time employees), we are talking about human beings who have been
performing specific functions. No matter where the individual goes (to
public services to give reference service in periodicals or to technical
services to manage the check-in of records on the automated system), there
has certainly been staff displacement. The old job no longer exists.

As professionals we must recognize the importance of addressing this
issue. We must look at the proposed system and talk about the new skills

needed to staff an automated circulation department. We must not assume that the individual who has been typing out fine notices by the thousands is going to adapt readily as a terminal operator. Jobs are often lost in the more routine areas of circulation to be replaced by higher skill requirement jobs. By the same token we have to analyze the impact upon the users who depended upon the public service function of the check-in clerk who actually handles the physical piece. That handling is all behind the scenes with shelvers transporting the items to the periodicals reading room. There may be an apparent loss of personal service if the planning hasn't included some attention to the users of the service.

It is now time to return to my initial thesis and develop some directions for successfully dealing with the technological present. If you recall I said the root of the problem is in "the political and ideological subordination of people" in the work environment and at the point of service. We must begin to involve our three constituencies at the point we begin to plan for new technology. One way of doing this is by establishing a team from the university administration, library employees and users (faculty and students). A clear set of goals and objectives can serve as a framework for the development of a comprehensive system or a single application. It is not important that all contingencies are addressed, but it is important to involve those to be affected by the changes.

A successful method has been to use this planning group to develop a rough outline of the areas to be addressed by technology and present a functional list of requirements. This list may be turned over to someone trained in writing functional specifications and who is knowledgeable about what is available in the marketplace. The resulting document is then presented to the planning group for review, and only after its approval are you ready to prepare a formal request for proposal (RFP).

This may seem like a time-consuming process, but it is well worth the effort. Since initiating the development of an RFP for a circulation system, I've been conducting RFP update sessions for interested staff (out of an FTE staff of sixty, I have had as many as thirty people attend these sessions). The first session covered basic automation, what it does, why we need it, and what it will mean in our library. The second session was a discussion of our RFP for a circulation system; basically, what are we asking for in a system. The third session was held once the RFP was sent to vendors, and it covered the next steps in the process of selection. We have now assembled an evaluation team consisting of university administrators, data processing specialists, library staff, and faculty. When a decision is reached, I will have another session with the staff discussing the selection process and answering questions about our choice.

This process has grown out of a firm philosophical commitment to the library staff and users. Design principles are important, but they must address more than file structures and screen displays. It is the successful combination of a good technological design with informed and interested library constituencies which will result in a model application of technology.

Another point at which subordination of library staff can spell failure is the implementation of a system. One suggestion is to establish an implementation quality control circle (QC) involving all those affected by the new system or subsystem. These groups should be voluntary and function statements should clarify the purpose of each group. QC skills should be acquired by the person facilitating the group and the group members should learn how they are to operate. A QC provides the mechanism for involvement of staff in solving problems at the very beginning and avoids the pitfalls of imposing technology on the workers. The worker "owns" the system at the outset and is less likely to sabotage. There is also peer pressure to have a smooth functioning system.

Thus far I have attempted to look at philosophical issues and practical solutions to technological problems posed for the multiple constituencies of the library. So what does all this have to do with professional competencies? Technological change has always produced more jobs than have been lost. They are often different jobs, in different places, requiring different skills.

I shall end my discussion by looking at a set of conditions which must be met if we, as information professionals, are to meet the demands of the information needs of society. In meeting those needs I hope we will be constantly aware of the technological present and avoid a fatalistic and futuristic confusion about technological development. Successful progress in library technology calls for a set of conditions to be met which are directly related to competencies:[8]

1. the library field must advance the technological state-of-the-art;
2. the professional work force must not become outdated in rapidly developing technological fields;
3. careers in library and information science must attract and retain intellectually able persons;
4. the paraprofessional work force must be trained to respond rapidly to the new tasks that the use of high technology products and services require;
5. the library user community, including the funding agencies, must understand the importance of investing adequately in appropriate technology to maintain a high level of information services; and
6. librarians must understand and contribute to policy issues relating to information.

Discussing these in more depth, first, universities must support research and development through the maintenance of strong faculties and state-of-the-art research facilities. Research must include the sociological and philosophical aspects of information technology.

Second, the problem of maintaining the major part of the professional work force at the state-of-the-art in rapidly changing technological areas is unsolved. While continuing education activities such as this are commendable, they do not provide an adequate solution to technological obsolescence of most library training. Major efforts by library schools and libraries will be needed to provide practicing librarians the skills needed to broaden and deepen librarians' knowledge bases throughout their careers.

Third, librarians and library schools must recruit talented individuals into the field. There must be incentives to retain the best and the brightest. We must offer challenge and opportunities for growth by increasing our visibility and image within society. We need technological competence and a philosophical understanding of the technology.

Fourth, paraprofessionals are an important part of the library work force. An adequate background in basic analytical skills will help individuals meet the demands involved in dealing with today's technology. Additionally, it is important for library administrations to invest the time and effort in training staff for the skills needed to perform complex operations.

Fifth, user communities must understand the importance of developing increased technological capability by setting that as a high priority with funding agencies. Librarians must become astute politicians so as not to set up a competitive environment for funding and technical resources. We must be able to demonstrate our ability to provide services to our entire population base—the development of library technology must be a common good. This is done by involving people, not just designing good systems.

Sixth, as librarians we must recognize the importance of the broader information community. We must become involved in the political process to ensure (1) that privacy issues are addressed, (2) that policy issues regarding the privatization of public information are made with the interest of public access assured, and (3) that a society of the information elite does not develop where only those who can pay for information get it.

It is an exciting future we have before us. We would be wise to think beyond our traditional roles to the broader contributions to the information community. We have skills which are needed, but we have been so tradition bound that we have looked at solutions too narrowly. The skills of traditional librarians combined with increased analytical skills will prepare us for important roles in the information society.

REFERENCES

1. Noble, David F. "Present Tense Technology." *Democracy: Journal of Political Renewal and Radical Change* 3(Spring 1983):8.

2. Bohr, Niels. *Essays, 1958-1962, on Atomic Physics and Human Knowledge.* New York: Interscience Publishers, 1963, p. 7. Cited in Bohr, N., *Atomic Physics and Human Knowledge.* New York: John Wiley & Sons, 1958.

3. Malinconico, S. Michael. "Planning for Failure." *Library Journal* 108(15 April 1983):798-800.

4. Wolin, Sheldon S. "Theme Note." *Democracy: A Journal of Political Renewal and Radical Change* 3(Spring 1983):7.

5. Noble, "Present Tense Technology," p. 8.

6. Ibid., pp. 10-12.

7. Ibid., p. 14.

8. List adapted from: Willenbrock, F. Carl. "Human Resource Needs for High Technology Industry." In *High Technology: Public Policies for the 1980s* (National Journal Special Report), edited by Richard S. Frank, p. 86, Washington, D.C.: Government Research Corp., 1983.

HILLIS L. GRIFFIN
Director
Technical Information Services Department
Argonne National Laboratory

Special Librarians Face the New Technology

As I tried to define the role of the special librarian for these proceedings, I recalled an experience that happened during a recent visit to London. We were walking through the tunnel under Oxford Street to Hyde Park at Marble Arch. As we emerged into the daylight we heard a terrible din, and we saw a busker shuffling along the path with instruments hanging all over him. Cymbals were between his knees, a drum on his back, a harmonica on a wire frame on his chest, and more besides! He was a one-man band. He was the whole show. The sweat was dripping off him, and he was doing his best under his heavy burden and the warm afternoon sun.

The Library Setting

Special librarians have some kinship with the one-man band. Although some special libraries have large staffs of experts in this or that field, most special libraries consist of the librarian who may, with some good fortune, enjoy the assistance of a clerk. Most special libraries are operated by one professional librarian who does the reference work, the cataloging, the book selection and the acquisitions, checks in the journals, answers the phone, tries to secure the return of books from reluctant users—and more, of course. These librarians must provide prompt, reliable, comprehensive, personal service to their users. They must find the answers—no fair pointing to the *Readers' Guide* or asking if they've checked the catalog.

There is a certain informality about the place and an absence of formal rules. People are dealt with on a personal basis, and the rules (if they exist at all) tend to be quite flexible. The next level of management, to whom the library reports, probably has no background in libraries or information work and therefore is often unable to appreciate the real needs (or triumphs!) of the librarian and the library, or to defend them properly against pressures to cut space, budget or personnel. The librarian often operates in professional isolation with little opportunity to share experience or questions with others, learn from them, or discuss professional matters. The daily give and take in a larger library, which enriches the daily experience, is often missing. Problems are often perceived as unique because there is no interaction with others in similar circumstances to provide the insight that the problems are common to all in these circumstances. The comfort and reassurance that it is not really anybody's fault, but simply the way of the world, is never received.

The coverage of the collections is often narrow in scope, but may be quite exhaustive in a given subject area. Unlike an academic library, the objectives of the institution and its staff are usually well defined, and the library does not have to be all things to all people. In some companies the objectives may change markedly and quickly, and the focus of the library collections must respond to these changes. This may require major changes in the subject content of the library, and major changes in the librarian's subject knowledge as well. The librarian may have to shuffle part of the old collection out the door to make room for the new. These changes cannot lag behind those of the organization if the library is to be an effective contributor to the organization's success in meeting its goals. The library collection may still be inadequate to its needs because of a limited budget, limited space, a limited time over which the collection has been developed, or even limitations in the number of people to identify, acquire and process the needed materials, or limitations in their skills.

A good special library has a certain tension in the air. It is not a passive place, waiting for the next person to happen through the door so that he can be pointed toward the card catalog or the pencil sharpener without disturbing the meditations of the librarian. There are places like that, of course, but we all know that they do their users and their sponsors a disservice.

Requirements of the Job

Special librarians play many roles in their libraries, and within the organizations that they serve. They need the professional skills of information science and librarianship to be self-supporting within the library. Although some feel that these can be learned adequately on the job, it is difficult to teach oneself these skills especially if one is running the library alone. Professional competence is very important to the special librarian.

Professional Skills

Professional skills in library and information science enable the librarian to identify, acquire, catalog, and retrieve the information needed by the users. These provide the librarian a background of reference resources and searching skills for use in finding answers. The whole framework of bibliographic organization is an important part of the library curriculum. Although some never comprehend it, the formal environment of the school of library or information science is where bibliographic organization is probably best synthesized and communicated.

Background Knowledge

Subject competence in the knowledge area served by the library is especially important. It enables the librarian to establish immediate credibility with the users of the library. It also enables productive communication with them at a level of equality and respect. If users feel that the librarian is simply the custodian of the collection (a clerical function), they will do for themselves and the librarian might just as well be a clerk. While subject competence can be learned in time, the game may well be lost if, by that time, the users pretty much ignore the librarian anyway except for the most trivial requests.

Keyboard Skills

Computer terminals are the order of the day. Every well-trimmed library is supposed to have one at the librarian's desk to bring those powerful databases to its door. Keyboard skills (the current euphemism for being able to type accurately at more than forty words per minute) open the world to the librarian. One of the great handicaps that many managers now have is that they cannot use the computer terminal effectively in their work because they cannot type. Keyboard skills are neither male nor female—they are a simple fact of life in the information age. Some of you may even know of people who are no longer effective in their positions within a library because they are unable or unwilling to learn to use a terminal to assist them in reference work, cataloging, or other library work.

Logical and Analytical Skills

Most of us came to librarianship from the humanities. The logical and analytical skills of science and engineering were not a part of that education. This is unfortunate, because these skills are important to success in library work. They are obviously the key to good cataloging, and to success in defining the reference question—i.e., helping the user to define what it *really* is that they are looking for. These logical and analytical skills are useful in developing the library's long-range plan, the budget or moving the collection. They may be coupled with skills in using a pocket calculator to arrive at the unit costs of alternative ways to do the same tasks in the library. They are another important set of skills that the librarian needs.

Searching

Searching is important in every aspect of the library. It follows from the logical and analytical skills which I just mentioned. But it now goes farther than that. Searching means the knowledge of how to use each of several online search systems in the most effective and efficient manner. One must know which system is best for one search, and which for another. Each system may have different operating protocols which must be learned, and each may organize the same information (e.g., *Chemical Abstracts*) in a different way, providing access in a different way on each system. A knowledge of how different files are organized, how different concepts are indexed in different databases, and which one to use for the best answer to the question at hand is vital. Let us not forget the real need for creativity here, so that when one search strategy fails you can come up with the one that *does* work.

Bibliographic Organization

Organizing and retrieving information are central skills in the library. In cataloging it is important to recognize new topics not adequately dealt with in the catalog, treat them correctly, and make them accessible to the users through adequate subject headings and cross references. In some situations, it may be necessary to do local abstracting and indexing to make information available for local needs. This is an expensive and time-consuming undertaking. Done poorly, it is useless. Skill in searching enables the librarian to see whether the subject is really not covered in the available databases, or whether it is merely hidden because the right search terms and strategy were not used. And, before I forget, an important aid to good bibliographic organization is a good memory. Have you ever noticed that some librarians never "see" the materials that come through the library, or the things that they read? But for those who do, isn't it a wonderful feeling to remember where you saw that "lost" fact when you need it? It's a sort of creative awareness. Some people turn off their minds while they are at work, so that they won't waste them or wear them out, I suppose.

Computer Skills

This is truly the computer age. Many of you have an OCLC terminal in your library, or a terminal to enable you to talk with the rest of the world.

Certainly the terminal takes a certain knowing technique, but after you've used it for a while you realize that nothing breaks when you hit the wrong key. There is an exactness about it—like following the rules and planning ahead. When we go further, and consider applying computer technology to the rest of the library, things change. We need to be conversant with the terminology and concepts of data processing just to be able to talk knowledgeably with others. But that is a skill that you need just to get along in today's world with its Apples and PCs and proliferation of other microcomputers. An excursion through a Data Processing 101 course (on a noncredit basis) will help if you don't expect it to cover library applications, and if you can stretch yourself to deal with a few very elementary accounting applications and square roots.

Computers on the Job

Librarians have to be able to deal with decisions about computers in their libraries. Do you need an Apple, a PC, or a computer at all? Who is going to write the programs and make it do the work? What work *can* it do? What work *should* it do, if any? Yes, "if any" because maybe you are better off without it, but need to be analytical, skeptical and perceptive to do the mental work to define all the ramifications of the problem and its solution. There are many useful computer programs for doing useful tasks. Just as you find answers for users of the library, you will have to find your own answers to what is usefully available in your circumstances. The librarian needs to be very sure that the word processing program is really necessary and efficient for the work to be done, that the spread-sheet program is really better than columnar pads and a big, soft, red eraser, and that the super database management system does not require that all authors, titles and subject headings be no more than ten characters long. It sometimes seems that we have a great reluctance, as librarians, to become knowledgeable about the most elementary aspects of computers and data processing. We need to view it as a tool for doing useful work, not as a tool for doing unnecessary work or for making existing tasks more difficult.

Management Skills

There are a group of nonlibrary skills that might be categorized as management skills, although they are somewhat broader than that. They aren't usually taught in library school, and in a larger library they would be the responsibility of the administrator, which is simply another hat that the special librarian wears. One is in the area of fiscal responsibilities— developing the budget by planning ahead, defending the budget, and managing within the budget ultimately assigned. Another is the area of personnel—i.e., planning, interviewing, training, supervising, and coun- seling are all necessary skills in keeping the library running. The librarian in this position must be able to get along well with others whether the people that they have to get along with are especially likable or not. Best of all, the librarians should be a practiced and astute politician who can sell the library program and its needs for money, personnel, space, and management support.

The Ultimate Skill

This is a long list of skills. Yet there is one that goes a long way toward overcoming any deficiences in that list. It is the personality of the person who works in the library. The library reflects that personality to the public. Nobody likes to deal with a frowner or someone with chronic (and vocal) depression. A warm, outgoing personality combined with professional skill and competence can make any library a success.

Where do the New Skills Come From?

Most of the skills that I have been discussing are not new to librarianship, nor are they unique to it. You don't have to look very far to see the human toll that has resulted from the advances in technology in only the last five years. Maybe some of you can even remember when the linotype operators and the railroad telegraphers (among others) thought that they were set for life—they would never have to change and their jobs would always be secure. There have been changes in the library, too. What about AACR2 and the ISBD; can one truly expect to build or use the catalog professionally in any library if these are foreign concepts to them? And there have been people who have not bothered to keep pace with the changes in their profession. They were not convinced of the need to change, and they were not convinced that they could do it. They felt that they could never adapt, learn, or master the new skills.

Where do the new skills come from? They come from reading the professional literature, and keeping up to date with what is going on in librarianship. It takes time to do that reading, but it is a necessary investment in retaining competence. And although some of it may take some thought and reflection, it is important to understand the issues and their implications.

Another source for acquiring new skills for the special librarian is the professional meeting. Professional meetings have a great deal to offer. The papers, seminars and workshops presented during these meetings are usually meant to be helpful in explicating new issues in the profession. The opportunity to converse about job-related topics with peers helps to make up for daily isolation on the job. Even the exhibits of the materials and services available from vendors show the direction in which things are moving, and often disclose a better or easier way to accomplish some task in the library. Too many of those who are responsible for the management of special libraries view meetings as a bagatelle, when in fact the practical and psychic rewards of attendance are significant. Subject-related workshops and seminars are more sharply focused, and provide similar benefits.

Continuing education was one of the original bases of the library—the working man's university. Many library schools offer continuing education courses at various centers around their state, at places convenient to those who would benefit from them, on topics of current utility, and at times and duration appropriate to the need. Many library schools which are located in metropolitan areas offer their courses during the late afternoon, in the evening or on Saturday, so that it will be convenient for those who already have their degree to update their skills and their minds. Rosary College, where I have taught for many years, is an example of such an institution. By the time most of us abandon the library at the end of a hard day, we are so tired that it is impossible to even *think* of attending a class at the local college, junior college, university extension center, or whatever. But continuing education is the lifeblood of professionalism in any field.

There is no shortage of things for the special librarian to do to keep up to date, current with the new world, and equal to the professional challenges of the library. It would be nice to have super-streamlined workshops, extension courses, seminars, journal articles, and picture books, that tell us just what to do—no thinking required. We would all like easy answers. We would welcome a "knowledge funnel" through which distilled wisdom could be poured into our heads. Whatever happened to sleep learning anyway—it sounded just like what we need, and so pleasant, too. Yet we can see that there is no simple way to keep current, and that everyone has to be a part of the solution. No workshop, book or seminar, no matter how well planned, publicized or presented, will help to bring this knowledge to us if we do not make our best effort to invest our time in professional growth and refreshment. And it is awfully difficult, when you are the one-man band, to quit beating your head against the drum, stop the music and take time to tune your instruments.

ACKNOWLEDGMENT

The author wishes to acknowledge the support for this project by the U.S. Department of Energy under Contract W-31-109-Eng-38.

LINDA BASKIN
Computer Coordinator
Illinois Cooperative Extension Service

MIMA SPENCER
Associate Director
ERIC Clearinghouse on Elementary and Early Childhood Education

Training Staff to Use Computers

Until recently, those who worked with computers were commonly thought of as having special knowledge or technical background not commonly known to others. In libraries the computers were likely to be managed by data processing staff only. Today, the idea of a single group "in the know" about computers is being replaced by the expectation that most of the staff in libraries and information centers will deal with computers in some form as a regular part of their work.

Advances in library automation are coming so quickly that administrators find that they are not able to wait for a new generation of staff trained in computer use or for the gradual spread of home computers to familiarize current staff with computers. The reality is that librarians and information specialists in the work force today will have to be trained to use computers on the job.

Inservice training on computer use can cover a wide variety of topics ranging from general information and awareness of applications to training on specific systems acquired by the library or information center. Training might be provided by a knowledgeable staff member or by an outside consultant or vendor. Whichever way is chosen, good training is crucial to the successful adoption of an automated system.

Although people have been using computers since the 1950s, it is only in recent years that large numbers of people unfamiliar with computers have had to be trained quickly and effectively for on-the-job purposes. Because of this need, there is growing interest in the processes of learning to use computers and in effective training techniques. Some questions being asked about training are: Can anyone who understands a computer system teach others about that system? Is teaching someone to use a computer similar to teaching other skills? What kinds of situations facilitate learning?

We have trained many different kinds of people to use computers for such applications as word processing, online bibliographic searching, file building, computer conferencing, software development, and accounting. Presenting numerous workshops and sitting in on sessions conducted by others have led us to believe that training staff to use computers is a complex process which is both similar to and different from other kinds of training. Inservice training on use of computers appears to work best when the trainer makes careful choices about the content of training and takes into account the kinds of experiences which help people learn about computers. Although in many situations the agenda of a training session is relatively straightforward (i.e., learn to use computer software, operate a computer or terminal), the best way to present what is to be learned, to introduce new concepts, or to schedule time for hands-on practice is usually less clear. Some suggestions and comments based on our experiences and analyses of the training process are presented in this paper.

HOW IS LEARNING TO USE COMPUTERS DIFFERENT FROM OTHER INSERVICE?

Time

One difference in learning to use computers as opposed to other kinds of learning is the greater amount of time necessary for trainees to absorb and integrate their new information with what they already know. Some people, often administrators, expect staff to be able to use a new computer system almost as soon as it arrives. Instead, in many cases there is a period of adjustment similar to that experienced by newlyweds, because in a way librarians become "married" to their computer systems, for better or worse, and need time in which to adjust to each other's peculiarities and capabilities. One reason this is true is that the cost of changing a computer system, once installed, is often prohibitive and retraining staff is time-consuming and expensive.

Training a staff to use a new computer system also requires more time than one might expect or plan for. One reason is the vocabulary that must be learned. Often the amount of computer jargon associated with a new system is confusing, particularly because terms such as *file, edit,* or *program* already have different connotations as they are used in daily speech. In many instances, the amount of time allocated for inservice on computers falls far short of what is needed even for trainees to gain a degree of awareness, much less have time to practice and develop proficiency in using the computer.

The difficulty in arranging for the amount of time needed to learn about computers, particularly time for hands-on practice, is compounded by the fact that computers are usually tied to a particular place (e.g., the office, a computer room, a terminal attached to a desk). Moreover, the computer may have to be used according to a particular schedule rather than when a trainee wants to practice. In many other kinds of training, materials can be taken home and studied at any convenient time. People learning to use office-based computers are not able to practice their new skills at home and so may learn more slowly than they might have otherwise.

Past Experience

Another thing which the trainer must take into account is the existing knowledge of computers the adult learner already has, which may include past experience and prior information about computers. Even adults with no computer experience will have formed impressions about computers from images of computers given in movies, television programs and articles, and from daily experience with computers in banks and stores.

Some of these impressions may be contradictory—e.g., consider the question of whether computers are portrayed as being active or passive. In some situations it is implied that computers are powerful entities having some degree of independent action, even volition. (The HAL computer in the movie *2001* is a case in point.) The image of an active, willful computer is also reflected in comments people make about how "the computer messed up my phone bill this month."

In contrast, people often hear that the computer is "a dumb machine that only does what it's told." The idea of such a passive computer may be less threatening, but it also implies that people who use computers need a high degree of technical knowledge. Many of these contradictory images originated in the early days of computer use when this was true— computers were housed in a sterile, isolated environment accessible only to technicians, scientists and engineers.

The increased use of home computers and experience with computers in everyday activities such as banking, travel and shopping is making people more familiar with what computers can do and with the meaning of terms such as *hardware* and *software*. Nonetheless, there is still confusion about the basic nature and capabilities of computers. Advertisements and articles freely use words and symbols such as *bit, byte, RAM,* and *K* without much explanation.

The trainer can probably anticipate many of the questions or misconceptions trainees will have about computers. In the area of microcomputers, for example, these kinds of questions recur: Do I have to learn to program to use a computer? How much math do I need? Can I use that disk in another computer? What is software exactly? How can we avoid breaking the computer? How much information can be stored on a disk?

To answer questions such as these, part of in service training may be devoted to a clear explanation of terminology and computer concepts, particularly those which may have been learned in other contexts (such as the word "file" which already has an office connotation). This explanation may set a tone for later explanations and should be extremely coherent and simple; not only is new information being provided, but trainees may be simultaneously sorting out or rearranging pieces of information acquired in other contexts.

Emotional Reactions and Concerns

Many adult learners are anxious or even fearful about computers partly because of the common conception of computers as powerful, difficult to use, and highly specialized—although at the same time fragile and expensive. These emotions may be intensely personal; a person may fear appearing foolish, being unable to learn the material, or causing damage to the computer. Comments such as: "I'm really dumb about computers," or "What kinds of things do people do that accidentally break the computer?" signal these concerns. Other people may express more general concerns about the effects computers will have on society, interpersonal relationships, or people's rights. ("Will people end up doing nothing but staring at computer screens all day? What information is stored in the computer?")

It is important for the trainer to recognize and address emotional reactions of anxiety and fear. This can be done directly by reassuring trainees that all people probably experience a degree of doubt or concern when trying to learn and practice a new skill and that most people, if not all, do in fact learn what is necessary. The trainer can also emphasize the idea that the current training is only a beginning, and that it is not necessary (or possible) to learn all about computers at once. This may be a good time to provide some background on the anticipated benefits of the computer system being taught—especially as to how it can save time or improve services—and to invite participants to exchange ideas about computers.

Interactive Nature of Computers

A great deal of the computer's power is derived from its potential to respond interactively to instructions or requests for information. Learning to take advantage of a computer's interactive capabilities may be a different experience for the new learner because casual observation of computer users on television and in stores or banks does not show the extent to which participation, choices and active involvement are required of any computer user. To many, the screen on the computer or terminal looks something like a television set. The keyboard resembles a typewriter. Neither of these familiar machines requires much response from its users—typing is essentially a one-way process and television is designed for a relatively passive viewer.

We have observed many new computer users typing in information or pressing keys without looking at the screen to get information on what to do next or feedback on what has happened. Similarly, the actions of a disk drive may seem to occur randomly or have no meaning to new users. The new user may try to proceed through a computer program without attending to these major clues as to what is going on inside the computer. In this situation, something as simple as an accidental press of a wrong key can cause unexpected results which may not be immediately noticed by the user. When the mistake or change is noticed, the user may be quite confused as to what has happened since he assumed (rather than saw) that everything was proceeding normally. Moreover, it may be difficult for him to retrace his steps and correct his error, which may in turn frustrate the user and give him the feeling that the computer is difficult to use. Once the interactive nature of the computer has been recognized, the user pays more attention to major clues such as changes or error messages on the screen. As a result, fewer frustrating situations are likely to occur; mistakes such as pressing the wrong key can be detected and corrected quickly.

The trainer can emphasize the interactive nature of using computers in many ways, for example, by making an analogy to driving a car which requires the driver to regularly make judgments and adjust to driving conditions. The trainer can even encourage beginners to look at the screen to see "where" they have been and to watch where they are going. When the trainer calls attention to clues on the screen and suggests how to interpret them, she helps trainees develop a habit that will lead to increasing independence and mastery of the computer.

HOW IS LEARNING TO USE COMPUTERS SIMILAR TO OTHER TRAINING?

There is nothing magic about teaching people to use computers; all of the techniques and principles that are helpful in other kinds of in-service training may be used. We have found, however, that some aspects of training need particular attention when doing training sessions on computers. These are discussed below.

Rhythm and Inservice

In any situation in which people are expected to learn new concepts and skills in a relatively short time, the participants tend to concentrate on the new information being presented and become intent on learning the task at hand. This intentness is essential for learning to take place. However, should this state extend beyond a certain point, it is likely to lead to a state of tension or stress which would be detrimental to learning.

Good training attempts to achieve a balance between the intentness associated with learning and fatigue-producing tension. Planning the training so that high concentration activities are interspersed with relief activities is one way to achieve a balance. This provides a certain rhythm of high and low points that allows more effective learning. It is important to note that learning can still take place during relief or "low" activity periods.

How can the concept of rhythm be applied to training? What kinds of factors are high concentration ones? Which factors should be considered as relief? Fatigue can be produced by participation in any kind of learning activity if it is continued past a certain point. This point might be called a satiation point. Some activities obviously produce fatigue more quickly than others. In our experience with different ways of learning, listening to a lengthy lecture or presentation must be classified as one of the techniques which produces fatigue the most quickly. However, any activity can be fatiguing if the practice goes on too long. In planning training sessions, especially those which are lecture oriented, trainers should take into account the rhythm of high and low concentration activities. Some of the factors which affect rhythm are described below.

Timing

No matter what kind of training is planned, timing and pacing are critical factors in the rhythm of training. For example, people cannot usually sit and listen to anything totally new, no matter how fascinating, for longer than an hour and a half. Even hands-on practice should not be continued for long periods without a break of some kind. After a period of intense activity, the satiation point is reached and relief is needed. The exact amount of time occurring before a satiation point is reached varies with individuals, kind of activity and particular circumstances (such as an overly warm room). It is the trainer's job to anticipate satiation points in the agenda based on the activities planned, knowledge of the group and his/her own experience.

Time of day is also a factor; morning is usually the best time for learning. After lunch people are often drowsy and training held in the evening is usually far less effective because of fatigue. These statements are not arbitrary but are based on likely events; an evening session will probably occur after a full day of work.

Variety

By deliberately varying the forms of instruction or kinds of learning activities, a trainer can provide relief while continuing to reinforce learning. For example, lecture, demonstration of software, film viewing, hands-on experience, and small group discussions are all modes of learning which can be either mixed or follow each other sequentially. Physically moving from one activity to another is beneficial to the person who has been sitting listening for a long while. In addition to varying the learning sessions, it is a good idea to intersperse learning activities with traditional "breaks" including a coffee break or a chance to browse through a display area, or to talk with other trainees.

Humor

A major form of variety often overlooked in formal training sessions can be provided by the use of humor. Humor is an element to which all audiences respond with relief. Learning tension is alleviated and trainees are more ready to learn after a good laugh. Appropriate anecdotes and witty comments or analogies can also help trainees remember concepts and relationships. The trainer must be careful not to overdo humor to the extent that trainees believe that content is neglected or their time is wasted.

Learning Styles

While sitting beside a swimming pool in Florida prior to a session on training people to use computers, we decided that there was an analogy between people's behavior at a swimming pool and various learning styles. At a pool, one person may dive in immediately, another may put in a cautious toe before walking slowly into the water, a third may jump in backwards, and a fourth may be pushed into the water. Just as these different approaches reflect different styles, some people learn about computers best by listening first, others by reading, still others by watching demonstrations or trying things for themselves.

Planning training to accommodate different styles of learning not only provides variety but also allows people to learn in the manner most comfortable and familiar to them. When possible, the trainer should offer similar material or present learning opportunities in a variety of ways rather than expecting everyone to learn from a lecture or from hands-on experience. For example, in setting up practice sessions with computer software, the trainer might try to arrange for an assistant to answer questions or offer a guided demonstration, set out handouts or manuals for those who want to see it in print first, and place signs beside the computer with step-by-step instructions for those who prefer to push buttons first and ask questions later. Those who are watching others should not be rushed to the keyboard until they have had a chance to absorb information. (The trainer will want to make sure they get a chance for hands-on experience and are not excluded by more assertive participants.) In addition to accommodating learning styles and providing variety, presenting material in a variety of ways is an opportunity for the trainer to repeat important information or reinforce material already learned.

Logistics

Although it may seem obvious, logistics can have a significant impact on the rhythm of the learning process. When logistics are a problem, they become an object of attention, detracting from trainees' concentration on the content. For example, it is best to try to avoid the need to rearrange the furniture to accommodate different activities such as lecture, small group, or hands-on practice. If the room is large enough (or a second room is available), the trainer can arrange to have areas set up ahead of time with chairs and tables in appropriate positions for different kinds of presentations. Computers should be in place and functioning long before the first person arrives for the training session.

THE INVISIBLE AGENDA OF COMPUTER TRAINING

In addition to the stated topics on the trainer's agenda (learn to use a circulation system, operate a word processor, etc.), there is an invisible, or less overt, agenda for in-service training. This invisible agenda has to do with such topics as helping trainees develop certain dispositions regarding computer use and encouraging habits which will lead to the trainees' continued progress in learning more about computers. Some ways to achieve this objective are discussed below.

Establish an Atmosphere of Receptivity for Learning About Computers

Especially in situations where inservice is required rather than voluntary, it is important to articulate to trainees good reasons for learning about computers. An opening discussion on the potential of computers to save time and energy or provide new and better services can carry people through initial frustrations they may feel during training. Using examples to relate computer capabilities to trainees' own work and providing reassurance to the group that everyone will learn what is required are also helpful. If enthusiasm and a sense of adventure are also part of training people will want to continue learning about computers long after a particular training session is over.

Perhaps most important in establishing an atmosphere of receptivity is the trainer's attitude toward the trainees. The trainees are adults who, although highly experienced in their work, may be in the position of being a "student" for the first time in many years. It is important for trainers not to talk down to them because they are in a student's role, but to value the vast amount of knowledge and experience they have and to draw on it.

Identify and Deal with Small Roadblocks to Learning

Learning simple processes such as how to turn on and off a computer or the proper way to insert a disk, or explanations of what the symbols on the keyboard really mean are examples of steps that should not be overlooked in the rush to get to the "meaningful" part of computer training. People's concerns that they may damage a computer or computer terminal must also be addressed. These small roadblocks may seem relatively unimportant, but understanding necessary procedures can give people a greater degree of self-confidence in using the computer on their own.

Make Sure Basic Concepts and Terms are Understood

Learning about a specific computer system may involve learning new computer terms and something about the way the computer works. Trainers should be especially careful to identify and define all of the terms associated with a particular program or application so trainees can follow the discussion. The technique of using an analogy to introduce a computer concept is one way to make an idea vivid so that it is easily remembered. For example, a computer program has often been compared to a recipe. Another technique for ensuring understanding of basic concepts is to encourage questions—especially those the trainee may consider "dumb" questions. The trainer can relabel the "dumb" questions as valuable and set up an atmosphere in which it is acceptable to admit not knowing something. If the trainer makes it clear that he/she doesn't have all the answers either, people will feel more comfortable about raising questions. If basic terms and concepts are learned during in-service training, the participants will be better able to continue learning than if they had simply memorized a set of procedures.

Be Aware of the "Critical Mass" Point

For many people there seems to be a point at which all the explanations, hands-on practice, and attempts to understand come together in a sudden feeling that they are beginning to learn about computers even if they have not yet mastered all of the details. All at once learning about the computer seems worth the investment of energy and effort. People vary widely in the amount of training necessary before reaching this critical point of understanding; some come to the training session with more experience or greater willingness to learn and others may be far from this point even after extensive training.

Although people vary in how quickly they move toward this point, it is clear that actual practice on the computer facilitates learning. Just as no one has ever learned to ride a bicycle by watching someone else ride one, hands-on experience with a computer is the only way to learn to use a computer. The intellectual understanding and awareness gained by demonstrations, lectures, etc. is valuable and necessary but no substitute for experiential learning. In the final analysis, each trainee must put it all together at the computer keyboard.

The job of the trainer might then be conceived of as arranging for the experiences most likely to move as many people as possible to the critical mass point. In order to reach this goal, the trainer must take into account all of the variables of training as well as the individual variability of trainees.

Identify Resources for Further Learning

Once the training sessions are over, the trainer may not always be available when computer-related problems occur on the job or when new information about the computer is to be learned. Therefore, in addition to learning basic concepts and procedures, trainees should also be introduced to resources that will help them learn more at a later time. For example, whether or not they will use it immediately, trainees need to become familiar with manuals on the computer system or specific programs. Other resources—such as a knowledgeable staff member or a "hotline" to technical assistance—provide ways for people to acquire new skills or to have specific questions answered.

Use Mental Models or Other Techniques Which Encourage Independence

Most of the above factors deal with making the trainees independent of the in-service trainer by encouraging them to continue learning on their own and providing the resources necessary to do so. Each trainer may have his/her own way of accomplishing this goal but one effective technique is to suggest that trainees make a mental model of the structure and options available in a computer system.

Mental models are based on the idea that in any interaction with a computer, the experienced user "sees" very different things than does a novice user. For example, when the floppy disk drive light in a microcomputer system comes on, the novice user sees a red light; the experienced user is more likely to "see" information flowing from the disk drive to the computer's memory. An experienced user of word processing may have a mental model of the program as a series of three boxes (a disk menu, an editor and a printing box) and use that image to keep track of "where" he is within the word processing program. The new user without such a road map may spend quite a lot of time memorizing each screen and appropriate responses at each of several choice points. In other words, much of the information flow within the computer system is invisible; the user cannot see most computer parts as he/she can when using a typewriter. Most experienced computer users know that some imagination and logical deduction is necessary, especially to figure out what went wrong in a particular interaction. Very few experienced users rely on memorizing a fixed set of responses when learning a new program. Instead, they are likely to construct a mental map or image of the new program as soon as possible.

Encouraging trainees to develop a mental model for a computer program or system can be a useful training technique. Modeling encourages people to analyze and understand what is happening within the computer. As they become more analytical, trainees begin to try to "figure things out" for themselves rather than seeking help for every problem. In other words, the mental model can provide a way for people to become more independent and confident about using computers.

Another reason for using mental models is that trainers, as experienced computer users, are often quite familiar with flow charts and similar diagraming techniques commonly used in computer programming and documentation and tend to present material from that frame of reference. They may therefore foster a strong orientation toward use of models, particularly diagrammatic charts. Whether or not trainees continue to use mental models as they learn more about computers, understanding how the trainer thinks about the computer program or system can often facilitate learning. When using his/her own model, the trainer may want to suggest that it is only one way of thinking about the program and that other ways will occur to trainees as they learn about the program.

TRAINERS AND THE COMPUTER MYSTIQUE

Knowledge of computers is a necessary but not sufficient qualification for an individual to be a good trainer. Almost on a par with subject expertise is the ability to translate computer concepts and operations into terms the trainees can readily understand. Those who are selecting a trainer may underestimate the value of this qualification since it is easy to be impressed by technical-sounding jargon and apparent breadth of knowledge. This phenomenon is part of the "computer mystique" that says computers are complex and difficult to learn and that one must be initiated into this arcane world by a sufficiently technical guide.

Anyone who teaches people about computers should be on guard against the computer mystique. A major goal of training should be to debunk the idea that one must be a computer scientist or mathematician to operate a computer. The trainer should strive to encourage people's confidence in their own ability to learn. At the same time, the trainer may want to set realistic expectations about what material trainees can learn during a given period and create awareness of what kinds of computer learning might require formal training in computer science.

Another facet of the computer mystique is the almost subconscious creation of an "in" group (those who understand) and a group on the outside. An expression of this subtle thinking is found in the trainer who refers to a topic as "more advanced" or "not for beginners." While it may be true, it does suggest a hierarchical, one-path system for learning about computers. A more helpful approach may be to use phrases that label the process rather than the person (e.g., "at the beginning" rather than "when you are a beginner"). The trainer can also indicate to trainees that there are many ways to learn about computers and different people start at different places and proceed along the path that suits their needs.

Another technique for avoiding the computer mystique is that of translating computer jargon into nontechnical phrases. The trainer can choose those terms that will be used during the training session. Terms to be used can be defined formally but also repeated several times in context as in "the program—the instructions for the computer—is found in...." All other terms which are not immediately relevant to the training session should be avoided or "translated" into nontechnical phrases. For example, the term RAM might be avoided and instead translated into a phrase such as "the computer's internal memory." With practice, trainers can do this translation quickly and easily and so avoid the excess of jargon that plagues many introductory sessions.

CONCLUSIONS

Awareness of the factors discussed in this paper is only part of the training picture. Integrating all of these factors is complex; the trainer must balance the needs of each person with those of the group, help trainees deal with anxieties or resolve prior misunderstandings while providing guidance and support for the new skills. A moment by moment response to unforeseen mishaps (what if the computer does not work?) and to the group's need to explore topics other than those on the agenda is required. Putting all of the pieces together for an enjoyable, well run session is almost an art—one which we are still exploring.

EVELYN H. DANIEL
Dean and Professor
School of Information Studies
Syracuse University

Education Matters

We have heard an interesting mix of practitioners and educators. My task today is to speak for library/information education in general. I hope you will consider my title, "Education Matters," to reflect both possible meanings. My comments will, no doubt, reflect certain personal and institutional biases, but fortunately there is in the audience a dean or two from other schools and a number of other educators who can leap in to contradict if I veer too sharply from the common path.

First, a digression. Dick Sweeney cautioned us not to let ourselves be defined by an institution or by a medium (as the book, for example). I agree with him. Clearly we are an information profession. We work with information in various ways and forms, with many different media, and in many kinds of organizations. We work with formal information systems and we create informal ones. The new information technology provides us with powerful tools that allow us to do these things more efficiently and also allow us to provide new services as well. We are all familiar with Gertrude Stein's quotation: "A rose is a rose is a rose!" However, I totally disagree with it. There is a lot connoted by a name. It affects our perceptions of ourselves as well as it does that of others. We need a broader view of our responsibilities. How many other professions do you know that are named for the place in which they work? We do not call doctors and nurses hospitalers; nor lawyers, courters (or courtpersons); nor do we call professors universarians. Why are we librarians? More and more we do not work in libraries. We work in technical information centers, in research and development, in information systems and marketing departments, and in a variety of other work settings, several of which José Griffiths mentioned in her paper. It is my habit to refer to our newly-defined field as the library/information field in order to link the old to the new in this transitional period. I will do this in my discussion.

I will talk with you first about education and change generally, articulating some of the problems both libraries and educational institutions have when facing a period of rapid, and perhaps revolutionary, change. I will describe three ways that library/information schools use in trying to accommodate for change. I will stress the importance of educators striving to articulate the future roles that librarians, other information workers, and information managers will have.

In order to be a bit more concrete and to provide some comment on the school librarians, or media specialists (as they call themselves)—a group without a speaker champion so far—the last part of my remarks will describe the newest addition to the competency-based school media program at Syracuse. This is a set of specific competencies for building-level computer coordinators in the elementary and secondary schools. There is a handout that lists these thirty-seven competencies that, with some misgivings, I make available to you now, although it would be nice if you would attend to me for the moment and read it later(see appendix A).

Still one more thing before I begin. I would like to comment—as most of the other speakers and many of the audience have also—on attitudes. My first proposed disssertation topic was a question relating to the desirability of selecting or devising some personality test to use to gather subjective data along with the more cognitively based evidence for admission decisions to library/information schools. I held the same strong feelings that have been expressed here about the need to screen out the more dull and lackluster of applicants. It was the first time I came to grips with the dangers of mission-oriented research. A good researcher must be neutral in the search for truth, prepared to accept and publish findings that may not be congruent with her personal and dearly held beliefs. Thus, I backed away from this research. Some corporations do use personality measures in selecting executives. At Syracuse, we use personal interviews, as do most schools, and although I make decisions based on these interviews, I am not prepared to defend them as objective. There appears to be some conflict, anyway, between whether traits of enthusiasm, creativity, alertness, and the quality of being energetic are enduring and consistent, or whether the situation in which one finds oneself has a greater impact on shaping personality. One psychologist says: "As we do, so we become." In other words, act enthusiastic and you become enthusiastic. In any event, for these reasons also, I chose not to do my research on this topic. In our school, and I think in most others, we focus on socialization processes to demonstrate the desired attitudes and to influence students to adopt those behaviors we believe are necessary in order to be successful in the profession. We counsel students who do not seem to fit to consider other career possibilities.

Beyond that it must rest with employers to make good selections and to act decisively in the probationary period if the needed qualities have not begun to emerge.

Now let me return to my main agenda. This conference has been devoted to examining the behavioral effects of the new technologies on the way we do our work in libraries—from a functional, institutional and attitudinal point of view. "Competency" has been used as a way to specify skills, knowledges and even attitudes. I believe the impulse to identify competencies and to develop a more competency-based education is directly related to the rate of change we face. It seems clear that we are entering a new kind of society based on information. This fact will impact all phases of life and create enormous dislocations. The changes brought forth by this revolutionary shift will be difficult to predict and virtually impossible to control.

How do we cope with this emerging information society and what does it mean to the library/information profession? In the past, libraries have performed a maintenance function for society. They have been responsible for the collection and preservation of recorded knowledge so that this knowledge can be passed forward to new generations of students and scholars both for direct application and as the basis for the creation of new knowledge. Education is also a conservative occupation. We conserve and maintain society's values and its knowledge base by packaging information into disciplinary chunks, by encouraging some people to devote their lives to the study and teaching of these chunks, and by creating institutions that provide structured ways to deliver smaller chunks—or packets of information—to students.

Both the library system and the education system work well in stable times. Both require large economic investments over long periods of time with anticipated payoffs even further in the future in various unspecified ways. Maintaining institutions do not work as well in times of rapid change. Old knowledge is not considered as valuable as new knowledge. A more superficial knowledge of several disciplines may provide better perspective than a narrow, in-depth single disciplinary focus. Technical knowledge seems more relevant than theoretical knowledge. Further, recorded knowledge seems less useful than information acquired directly from the environment. Recorded knowledge appears to be more difficult to assimilate than spoken information received through social contacts.

The first question then is how can the library/information profession absorb societal change, reexamine its mission, realign its priorities and its central tasks to remain relevant and perhaps even become central in this emerging information age? The second question is how can an appropriate education system be devised to suit the needs of a dynamically changing profession in a dynamically changing world? I will briefly comment on three models for change in library/information educational programs. For brevity, I have labeled these three models incremental, conceptual/futurist and skill-oriented.

The first approach is the model of incremental change. In this model, we recruit new faculty from different backgrounds. We revise curriculum, add courses in new areas, and perhaps even add a few new topics to existing courses. We purchase a piece or two of new equipment. We make change gradually and perhaps a bit cautiously. The attitude is reactive and defensive. Many library schools have adopted this approach almost by default. I understand and sympathize with this decision (or nondecision). However, unless the pace of internal change matches the pace of change in the surrounding environment, this approach will probably not succeed.

Another model involves a more activist stance on the part of the educational institution. I have called this model conceptual/futurist. Predictions are made about the shape of the future and the kind of work that people will do. A new field is delineated or, at the very least, the old field is radically redefined. A number of schools have taken this approach. In one of the more extreme, Pittsburgh maintains a separate information science department with a distinct curriculum and a different faculty from that in the library science department. We at Syracuse have attempted to grapple with the meaning of the information society and how it affects those of us in library/information work. We define the mission of our field as the facilitation of information use by humans. We believe that this mission is enduring and continuous, but the manner in which it is accomplished is becoming radically different and highly various. The nature of the change is such that we believe we must become more academic and questioning in our approach to education as opposed to a professional, prescriptive orientation. We cannot specify "best practice" with the same degree of certainty and authority that we could in more stable and predictable times.

Still a third approach involves the abandonment of the broad view and the long view. Here little attention is paid to theoretical frameworks and comprehensive models. Rather, the focus is on what is happening now, today, out there in the field on the front lines. This is the practical orientation of the engineer rather than the objective and neutral approach of the scientist. The curriculum for this approach manifests itself in highly specific courses—often skill-based and occasionally context-based. An example of the former is a programming or an online searching course; an example of the latter is a course in managing an information service business (we offer all three courses at Syracuse). In this skill-oriented model, many faculty are drawn from practice and teach on a part-time basis. The education function moves closer to an apprenticeship experience rather than an academic one.

None of these approaches are satisfactory by themselves. Fortunately, there are few examples of any of the three in pure form. We educators all hedge our bets in a variety of ways. We use modifications and amalgamations of all three approaches. The competency-based approach to education may be one tool to help accomplish this.

Remember the task of the library/information school is to predict the need and to devise a means of meeting that need. The resources that we hold are the curriculum (what Les Asheim calls "the major academic device educators have for confronting society's challenges...."), the faculty, the available space, facilities and equipment, and ultimately, the budget which makes possible all the other resources.

Going back to the three models, although we might wish to rule out the incremental approach because of its slowness, in fact we exist within a university which is also a maintaining, conserving institution which moves deliberately and a bit ponderously where change is concerned. It is difficult to effect change rapidly in universities. There are several bodies that must review and approve curriculum change. Faculty also change slowly over time. They must first be convinced of the need for change and then be given time and resources to develop new capacities and to attain new knowledge. Facilities have to be redesigned and new technology acquired. This usually involves renovation—and it all takes money. New money is scarce so it becomes a zero-sum game. Decisions have to be made within the school and within the university on where cuts can be made and how funds can be reinvested in new ways. This requires much justification and many persuasive arguments within the school, within the university, within the professional community, and within the prospective employer community.

Thus, even for incremental change to take place, a new vision of the field must emerge and be articulated. This brings us back to the second approach. We *all* must concern ourselves with the meaning of the information society, the implications it holds for the way people do work and interact with each other, and how this affects and shapes the information profession. Technology is pushing us into this brave new world of the future. For example, here are some speculations and predictions from a recent presentation on videodisc technology and its impact on libraries. These are six from a very long list.

1. High density storage media will replace books as the primary method for storing and recording knowledge. Microforms never really accomplished this, but videodiscs probably will.
2. The collection and storage function of libraries will become independent of the searching, locating and retrieving. They no longer have to co-exist within one building.

3. The technical aspects of information work will dominate over the more intuitive aspects.
4. Search systems will be designed for end users rather than intermediaries.
5. Libraries will become centers of instruction, of testing and, perhaps, for presentations.
6. There will be fewer specialized libraries and fewer special collections in libraries. (Edward Schneider. "Videodisc Technology." Presentation at the Spring Conference, School of Information Studies, Syracuse University, Syracuse, N.Y., 22 April 1983.)

I could give you further speculations and predictions about the impact of the computer and telecommunication technologies, especially about the fifth-generation logic machines, but these are more familiar areas for all of you. (In passing, let me note the distinction between speculations and predictions. Speculations are those assertions you disagree with; predictions are those with which you agree.)

We who are educators are paid by society to study, observe, test, think, and write about things in ways that practitioners with immediate operational urgencies cannot allow time for. Thus, it seems clear that we educators have a responsibility to attempt formulations of the future role or roles of the library/information professional. Our knowledge base for these formulations comes from a variety of sources—e.g., writings from an array of disciplines, journalistic comments and reports on new developments from the popular news media, observation of current practice, laboratory simulation of possible activities, empirical research, and discussions with people in the field and in related fields.

One thing is obvious. We must close the gap between town and gown as much as possible. We already have a number of mechanisms to maintain currency about present practice. We invite guest speakers from the practice world to come to our classrooms to talk about how it really is. We take students on field trips. We develop internships and other practicum experiences for students. We create advisory councils. These activities are essential in order to assure relevancy for a changing profession.

In discussions between practitioners and prospective employers on the one hand and faculty on the other, it sometimes appears the two groups speak at cross purposes. Practitioners often want to know why there are not three or four specific courses of increasing sophistication in their specialty taught by a full-time faculty member who is a recognized expert in that particular area. Thus we might have, for example, a series of courses on the acquisition of government documents, classification and arrangement of document collections, information retrieval from these collections, a course on government dissemination of information, and the like—all of which are perfectly reasonable courses and would be very thorough preparation for documents librarians. However, what about the educational needs of the serials librarians? Or the archivists? And what about all the other subspecialties within our field? And, of course, there are the traditional specialties of academic, public, and special librarianship—the latter in all its many manifestations.

In my hypothetical list of specialized courses for the documents librarian, we can observe that all of these areas are concerned with some aspect of information processing—i.e., selection, acquisition, collection, storage, retrieval, and use. Managing collections and providing information services are concerned with planning, organizing, staffing, monitoring, reporting, and evaluating. The medium may be different, the context may be different, but the functions and the processes are the same. Most educators believe a function- and process-based curriculum is more basic, fundamental and generalizable than a context-, medium- or mission-based one. It is more effective for students to learn to apply general principles to new situations.

Because of this difference in perspective, discussion between practitioners and educators often fails to connect. For good communication to take place and for the practitioner to impact the curriculum, a shift in attention from a concentration on inputs (courses and faculty) to outputs (expectations and detailed descriptions of desired outcomes) becomes a potentially fruitful strategy. To describe particular positions in terms of the competencies required to perform essential tasks can be very helpful to educators. This approach might also be a useful device for practitioners in a systems-analytic way to enhance their own understanding of the role they play.

A list of desired competencies for a specific occupation, along with a general position description (or role conceptualization, as we educators are wont, somewhat pompously, to say) can be a good tool for faculty to examine whether or not a competency can be attained and demonstrated within the existing courses, whether a new course is needed, whether a specialized independent study may be necessary for those cases where there is only a small demand, or whether special field work must be tailored for the student when the competency is such that it can only by attained or demonstrated in field-work settings.

Competency lists are highly useful for other reasons. A person engaged in career planning usually wants more specific information about what he/she would actually be doing when he/she becomes a systems analyst—for example, for an academic library. Similarly, the person planning to make a career shift can examine the competency list to see where strengths already held can be exploited in new ways. The independent learner who cannot afford (or does not choose) to attend a formal education program can use the competency list as a guideline and road map for self-study. Competency lists can be useful aids for continuing-education providers and consumers.

Thus there appears to be great utility in developing a set of behaviorally-oriented competency statements for subfields within the library/information profession. However, I hasten to add that these competency sets must always be treated as incomplete and unfinished. These lists must be amended, modified, added to, and deleted in a continuing process. This can be fairly easily accomplished once they exist in some published or semipublished form. Computer-generated word processing and text editing are ideal for these constantly changing documents.

To summarize and provide a more concrete example at the same time, let me briefly describe our experience at Syracuse with a competency-based curriculum for school media specialists. This is a joint program between the School of Information Studies and the Department of Instructional Design, Development and Evaluation in the School of Education. Don Ely (from Education) and I have written fairly elaborately of the process we went through, but I can summarize it in five sentences. We brought together a consortium of practitioners, employers, educators, and students. After a series of long and argumentative meetings, we reached consensus on a set of seventy competencies. We devised a course-by-competency matrix to identify where (or if) each competency was taught and could be demonstrated. With faculty review and approval, we modified existing courses and developed an advising procedure to lead students through the matrix maze. We hold an advisory group meeting once a year to review and amend the competency list and to assess how well it is being implemented within the curriculum (see appendix B for a partial list of competencies included in the program). We are in our fifth year of the program. There have been a number of changes, but we are more and more satisfied with this approach and with the performance of the students graduating from it.

We liked the process and the outcome so much that we decided to replicate it on another subspecialty. We observed that public schools are purchasing microcomputers and software on an increasing scale but with very little systematic planning. A possible role for a building-level computer coordinator began to be discussed. Various individuals have assumed this role in a part-time way, based mostly on personal interest, previous background, and occasionally simply due to arbitrary assignment. Good school librarians tend to be educational leaders, generalists and often opportunists. Many of those who like to be where the action is began to reach for the role of computer coordinator for their buildings—writing grants; selecting hardware and software; organizing schedules for use; working to develop computer literacy curricula; leading workshops to train teachers; and seeking ways to become connected to the outside world via the use of a micro simulating an intelligent terminal; or speaking to a mini- or a mainframe computer at the district level, to bibliographic utility networks, or to other databases like the Source or CompuServe. Our advisory council suggested that the School of Information Studies develop a program and stake a claim on the educational preparation for this role.

We selected two library media specialists who were on the cutting edge of this new field and were already heavily involved in a variety of computer-related activities while at the same time carrying on exemplary programs. We also chose a superintendent who needed a bit of convincing at first but became our most enthusiastic supporter. We added a regional level information systems supervisor who was a bit dubious of the librarian's abilities in this area but who also came around. Other participants were a couple of educators and the Director of the State Center for Learning Technologies. The latter traveled from Albany to Syracuse for the four meetings because of his belief in the importance of this effort. Again, we debated and argued quite vigorously, often taking classic postures of "theoretical academic" *v.* "practical librarian." We did reach agreement on what we believe is an acceptable set of thirty-seven competencies, which I share with you today (see appendix A).

I will not take time today for a detailed walk-through except to note that these competencies are listed in the reverse order from the way we developed them, and probably in the reverse order from the way they would be attained. We arranged them to go from general to specific in the document for a better conceptual presentation. In general, students first acquire those competencies listed under *Hardware/Software Selection and Development,* then the ones itemized under *Organization, Information Provision and Teaching.* They tend to learn last those listed under *Supervision/Coordination/Management* and *Communication and Leadership.*

We will use this list in a number of ways. Internally it will help us realign our curriculum. We have still to agree on the broad position description statement. Once we have the three pieces in hand—the job description, the competency list, and the description of the necessary educational preparation—we will create a small brochure outlining the program, which will be mailed to interested parties. We are working on a road show to present the program to superintendents, principals and school board members for feedback and visibility. We are also working with the state certification department to achieve recognition of the role either as a separate certificate or as part of the general media specialist certificate. We will develop a three or four course sequence as a continuing education program for those in the field who want it. And, of course, we will integrate these new competencies with the existing ones for entering prospective school media specialists.

Many of the competencies listed here, especially those on the last page under *Hardware/Software Selection and Development* (the more specific and technical), are applicable to a variety of other information positions. In fact, a cursory examination shows that all of the competencies listed here are presently taught in our curriculum somewhere. They may not be packaged appropriately or emphasized sufficiently for the new program but the accommodation process should be relatively easy.

By this time in the conference, I anticipate that we may have over-stressed the competency aspect so I will not belabor it further but end by trying to summarize the advantages and disadvantages of the competency-based approach for education. The advantages are that it makes a fine communication device for practitioners and educators to talk to one another; it leads to a more relevant curriculum; it describes outcomes in observable, behavioral terms; it allows people to attain competencies in a variety of ways not always through formal education; and it is easy to maintain currency. However, there are disadvantages. It is nontheory driven. Even though our programs are professional (to reiterate) it is difficult to impossible to specify "best practice." We all need to become more academic in our approach. This is true for practitioners as well as educators. A competency-based curriculum tends to focus on what *is*, rather than on what *might be*, although it might have elements of aspiration in it. Finally, and perhaps related to the lack of theory and the omission of the old term *understanding of* as a goal statement at the beginning of a course, I believe that integration and the holistic overview of the profession may suffer under a completely competency-based approach.

Still, if we truly believe in a lifelong learning, we should apply what we know about how people learn. We know that they want to learn first how to do it and where it will be done—skills and context. New graduates on their first job invariably complain that their school did not give them enough practical training. In five to ten years, their plaint is that the school did not pay sufficient attention to management and supervision. Ten to twenty years later, they complain that we did not provide enough theory and philosophy. A reasonable solution might be to provide education at several levels and kinds throughout the professional career of practitioners.

There is much, much more I would wish to talk about but too much time has passed already. Let me leave you with the definition of the future by Ambrose Bierce. He said: "The future is that period of time in which our affairs prosper, our friends are true, and our happiness is assured." May it be so for all of you!

APPENDIX A

Competencies for the School Media Specialist
Relating to Building Level Computer Coordination

Developed by the School Media Specialist/Computer Task Force, School of Information Studies, Syracuse University, 18 April 1983

Communication and Leadership

1. Describe the leadership role of the media specialist and strategies for implementation of such role in relation to a school's movement in the technology area.

Supervision/Coordination/Management

2. Participates with teachers and administrators in establishing the instructional computing plan.
3. Develops policies and guidelines for computer resources based on established goals and objectives.
4. Considers the requirements of instructional computing when planning media facilities use and allocation.
5. Seeks unique fiscal arrangements beyond regular budget sources including multiple sources of support.
6. Serves as a liaison between building, district, regional agencies and other related organizations to the school.
7. Determines appropriate uses of computers in media management tasks (i.e., acquisitions, technical processing, circulation, inventory, budgeting, and planning).
8. Coordinates (schedules, allocates, oversees) the implementation of the instructional computing plan.
9. Assists teachers in using computers for classroom management tasks.

Teaching

10. Establishes user training standards to minimize risk to both users and hardware/software.
11. Teaches the basics of using computers to students, teachers and staff.
12. Coordinates continuing education/in-service instruction for teachers.
13. Assists students and teachers in using/troubleshooting CAI programs.
14. Uses CAI materials in library media skills instruction.

Information Provision/Curriculum Integration

15. Provides access to sources of information regarding hardware/software in-service opportunities and applications.
16. Provides access to online databases as appropriate to the curriculum.
17. Analyzes and evaluates the curriculum in order to recommend and provide appropriate automated information sources.
18. Participates in K-12 computer literacy curriculum development.

Organization

19. States the laws and regulations regarding copyright, patent and duplication.

20. Describes the special problems associated with the organization, storage, retrieval, and distribution of computer software/hardware.
21. Specifies conservation, care, maintenance and storage mechanisms for hardware/software.
22. Repackages materials into efficient formats and carriers appropriate to particular needs.
23. Develops distribution/circulation policies and procedures appropriate to the nature and use of hardware/software.
24. Identifies and evaluates sources of information for selection and acquisition purposes.
25. Acquires hardware/software locally ("homemade"), commercially, and through contracts and licensure agreements (see also appendix B for existing organization competencies).

JULIE CARROLL VIRGO
Executive Director
ACRL

The Role of the Association
in Developing Professional Competence

I would like to begin by reviewing what it is about an association that shapes the special role it can play in developing professional competence. To begin with what is perhaps the obvious, a professional association consists of a group of people who identify with a particular profession.

The *Encyclopaedia of the Social Sciences*[1] defines a profession as an occupation requiring intensive and continuous preparation. In searching back in my memory to library school classes, I remember the characteristics then cited to describe a profession:

1. it has a body of knowledge that describes the field and some consensus about that body of knowledge;
2. it requires extensive study or preparation;
3. there develops a commitment to training new entrants and extending the knowledge;
4. it develops a body of literature and the publication of scholarly journals to disseminate the information; and
5. groups are formed to advance the goals of the profession—in other words, the development of associations.

Characteristics of an Association

Reviewing the characteristics of an association that will influence the roles it can assume within its profession, it is apparent that an association:

—has access to a large number of people in the profession;
—is a body of people who collectively have a tremendous wealth of experiences to draw upon in a common field;

—has access to pooled funds (from membership dues and other revenue sources) to attack problems that are industry wide and which may be too expensive for any one institution to deal with;

—can influence entry into the profession, and the education of those in the profession, because of its concern with professional practice;

—can set general standards for the performance of its members, by the promotion of statements such as "Codes of Professional Ethics, which keep before us the ethical implications of allowing the obsolescence of professional skills...";[2]

—develops journals and a literature for disseminating developments in the field;

—attracts a significant mass of the profession whenever it holds meetings, be they national, regional or local;

—can speak on behalf of the profession in presenting a unified voice on issues affecting the profession; and

—is perceived by outside groups as a voice of legitimacy and authority about issues and matters relating to that profession.

Roles Played by Associations

Taking advantage of these characteristics, an association can develop the competencies of members of that profession by executing a variety of roles. Examples of these include the following.

An association can highlight "good" or innovative practice, so that the practice can be viewed as a role model for other libraries to follow. Examples of such practices and how they have been highlighted are discussed below.

—The Literature-Attached-to-Chart (LATCH) programs where a packet of relevant current medical articles is attached to the patient's medical record so that each person on the health care team treating the patient has easy access to the latest published information about that particular disease or pathology. The LATCH program was highlighted in the Medical Library Association's twenty minute movie *Rx Information— The Health Sciences Library.* This film has been used in teaching library school students, as a discussion film with an accompanying guidebook at library meetings throughout the United States and abroad, and in promoting innovative library services with hospital administrators and medical staff.

Similar examples can be cited for other types of libraries. Peggy Sullivan's ALA film *Libraries and the Pursuit of Happiness* shows libraries and librarians playing a variety of innovative roles for their user groups.

—Model bibliographic instruction programs in academic libraries of all types have been replicated more quickly around the country as a result of the publicity given to such programs through association journal articles, speeches at library association meetings and handbooks published by the Bibliographic Instruction Section of the Association of College and Research Libraries.

—By highlighting the cost reduction programs at the libraries of the Claremont Colleges in California, where significant savings have been made by thoughtful substitution of technology for labor, other libraries and librarians are able to explore if such an approach, or a modification of it, might be applicable in the way they practice librarianship in their own institutions.

Highlighting innovative or special practices encourages not only library staffs to emulate newer developments, but also makes their user and funding audiences more aware of the capabilities of their library resource. This in turn can encourage professional development as the library staffs respond to increased user expectations.

An association can influence the development of professional competence by *setting educational standards* for the profession. This may be done in the formal basic education programs such as the accreditation program administered by the Committee on Accreditation of the American Library Association. Or, another approach taken by some library associations, most notably law and medical ones, has been the development of certification programs that may be used by employers as a requirement for certain positions, usually entry ones. The Medical Library Association has gone one step further by requiring continuing education or reexamination as a necessary requirement for recertification.

An association can provide an environment where *leadership and group skills can be developed* through committee work and governance structures. This is particularly important for librarians who work in small organizations where other opportunities for the development of these skills may not exist.

In some circumstances association committee work can also provide opportunities to *learn new technical skills or knowledge* as part of particular association assignments. For example:

—Editors of journals and newsletters learn about the publishing process.
—Assignment to a Budget and Finance Committee may be a person's first experience at dealing with an organizational budget. He/she may have to learn how to read balance sheets and income statements, and the importance of cash flows despite an accrual accounting system.

—Developing new standards—such as the Z39 committees or developing a new cataloging code—will teach a committee member the finer points about very technical subjects.

—Working on an association conference can bring insights to the behind-the-scenes activities of hotels, convention centers, exhibits, contracting for social events, and organizing and implementing publicity campaigns.

—One committee I am working with at the moment is learning about the costs and feasibility of developing and producing a machine-readable database that will ultimately become the third edition of *Books for College Libraries*. This has required the committee to gather and analyze data from OCLC, from vendors and database producers, to conduct pilot tests in their own libraries and, in sum, learn more about database construction, publishing and production than any of them would ever have had an opportunity in their own libraries.

—My ACRL president-elect suggested I mention to you another competence she has developed by participating in the association—a working capability with electronic mail. While it was technically available in her own institution, she had not previously used it until she served on the governing Board of ACRL where the decision was made to experiment with electronic mail.

Because an association has the capability of pulling together a body of librarians at its national, regional and local meetings, it provides an opportunity for the *exchange of ideas* and the resolution of professional problems. A person working in a small library setting needs to hear about how things are done in other libraries. And librarians who work in large organizational settings have a similiar need to mix so that they do not become parochial and insulated in their view of the world they serve.

An association has natural *mechanisms for disseminating information* in a variety of formats that transcend space, time and geography. Its meetings provide a forum for the exchange of ideas, the presentation of papers, and an opportunity to learn about new products and services from advertisers and exhibitors. The meeting programs may be subsequently published, may be available on audiocassette, or even teleconferenced from the site of the meeting for those people who are unable to be physically present.

An association usually publishes at least one journal in which research and practice can be disseminated to the profession. Most associations have also developed publications programs for the distribution of monographs, handbooks, checklists, and nonprint materials. Each of these activities has as one of its goals the increase of knowledge or competency of those who use the materials.

An association can engage in *projects that are aimed at improving professional performance* but that are too costly or impossible (for reasons other than cost) for any one individual library to conduct. Several examples come to mind. In medical librarianship, the membership of the Medical Library Association decided that it was important to identify the competencies needed to be a "good" generalist medical librarian. Such a project could not be carried out in any one medical library because:

1. it would be too costly, if done using generally accepted methodologies;
2. the competencies identified could not be directly extrapolated to all types of medical libraries (hospital, medical school, big, small, special) and to all regions of the country, nor even to another similar medical library which had different procedures; and
3. such a study would be less likely to be viewed as credible without the reputation of a more broadly based body behind it.

In academic librarianship the decision was made to promote the concept of bibliographic instruction with subject discipline associations. A comprehensive plan was developed to get faculty members to speak on the programs at the conferences of subject discipline associations around the country. In addition, traveling exhibits were developed to be used at these meetings, and a variety of materials were prepared for distribution. A project of this nature, which aims to enhance the academic librarian's participation in the student's education, may be an activity which an individual institution may feel is sorely needed, but no one institution could justify organizing speakers at fifty-seven subject-discipline associations around the country in order to get its own faculty and librarians to work together in new and different ways to improve the student's educational experience.

Most of the programs developed by the Office for Management Studies of the Association of Research Libraries would also fall under this rubric. The development of the methodologies used in the Management Review and Analysis Project, the Academic Library Development Project, and the Collection Analysis Project would have been extremely expensive if only applied to a single library. By funding the development of the methodology collectively through membership dues and grants, many libraries were able to benefit from these studies that would otherwise have been unavailable to them.

In sum, an association has access to pooled funds to attack problems or challenges that are industry wide but which may be too expensive for any one institution to deal with.

A final role on my list of those roles an association can play in developing professional competence is the one which may have been the first to occur to you—the role of the association as a *provider of continuing education programs.*

A survey done in 1975[3] showed that library associations were the largest single provider of continuing education programs, accounting for 28 percent of the courses offered in that year. While that percentage has probably decreased over the past eight years, library associations of all types still account for a significant proportion of continuing education courses.

Associations at each level have important and distinct roles to play. Quoting from Barbara Conroy, library associations are:

> Primarily responsible for identifying the larger learning needs within the library field. Often in the best position to look ahead at tomorrow's needs as well as those of today, associations organize and implement efforts to desseminate new information and produce new skills. This includes committing conference time and resources for learning purposes as well as establishing committees and assigning staff with specific responsibilities for continuing education. By making information, access and opportunities available, they can encourage active participation of their members in learning activities. They establish standards and guidelines for learning opportunities, produce journals and publications, and identify resources to help practitioners learn.[4]

Local associations, aimed at small geographic concentrations, are likely to become increasingly important given today's economy. An article discussing the advantages of local associations stated:

> The local association has several distinct advantages over regional or national associations in preparing programs or workshops. One advantage,... is familiarity with the audience—their backgrounds and levels of experience. Second, the...local association can tailor its programs to the specific needs and interests of its membership...because committee members are physically close together, it is easier to plan and coordinate a program. The cost should, of course, be less when committee members do not have to make long-distance telephone calls or travel [far] to other towns. In addition, committee service and program participation at the local level can provide excellent opportunities for younger librarians to develop skills (e.g., organizational and public speaking skills) that readily transfer to service in larger organizations.
> [While] the local association...[will] never replace regional or national associations..., it can provide supplemental enrichment especially in times of tight budgets, when travel money is scarce.[5]

National library associations are able, on the demand of their membership, to develop courses and put them on in different parts of the country. Research has shown that librarians generally are able to get release time more easily for conferences than for short courses. The association which conducts continuing education courses in conjunction with its conference may be able to attract registrants for whom permission to attend a conference in more readily available.

In assessing the problems, challenges and constraints on the association's role in developing professional competence it may be helpful to review what we know about the attitudes and economic/social/political environment as they relate to librarians and professional development.

From surveys of librarians[6] we have some data on how librarians view continuing education, what motivates them to participate and what factors are deterrents. "Librarians with higher career aspirations are more likely to support and take advantage of continuing education opportunities[7]....Librarians...viewed continuing education as a source of more effective job performance, challenge, creativity, and satisfaction...."[8]

As deterrents, they indicate "lack of time...as the prime deterrent, followed by prohibitive costs...."[9] Allie Beth Martin and Maryann Dugan, in their study, found that insufficient time and money were major frustrations for libararians interested in pursuing continuing education.[10]

In a study of health sciences librarians by John Naisbitt,[11] it was found that people who received no paid release time nor financial support to attend meetings or courses attend few of them. For those working in smaller library situations where no one can cover their jobs for them, it is difficult to obtain release time.

A survey of academic libraries recently found that virtually all academic libraries provide some degree of assistance to their staff members for attendance at library conferences and continuing education activities.

> Among the...libraries [surveyed] 98 [percent] make available at least partial support for staff travel to meetings and workshops. Ninety [percent] help defray the costs of hotels and meals; ninety-seven [percent] provide funds for registration...;and...100 [percent] allow released time for meetings and continuous education. Forty-eight...[percent] offer at least partial tuition reimbursement for library-related academic courses.[12]

Turning to considerations of what kinds of professional development experiences librarians prefer, it was found from the Neal study:

> All the librarians surveyed were involved in both formal and informal activities, with books read and course work in a subject area, and association membership and conference participation in librarianship clearly favored...." "[They] viewed the interaction and self-study modes as being best suited to their needs, objectives, and job demands...."[13]

Another study by Virgo asked: "Briefly describe the most meaningful professional learning experience you have had in the last year."[14] The results showed that the response rated most frequently (twice as frequently as the next most frequently rated response) was "on-the-job challenge or problem solving experience." The results were:

—On-the-job challenge or problem solving experience	32%
—Group learning experience (for credit)	16%
—Individual learning experiences	14%
(writing papers, preparing a course, planning and	
pursuing a sequence of activities of self-instruction)	
—Professional meeting	11%
—Group experience (noncredit)	11%
—Discussion with colleague	7%
—No answer	9%
Total	100%

It seems that those surveyed found most meaningful continuing education through practical experience, an assumption common in other areas of adult education.

During the past ten years, there has been a tremendous increase in the number of continuing education courses being offered by all continuing education providers. Recent data tend to indicate the market for association courses as we presently know it may be becoming saturated (and now I am referring only to the short workshop type courses). While the number of course registrants may have increased slightly, we are seeing that the association-sponsored courses are attracting fewer registrants.

This may be a result of two factors. A declining economy may have impacted on the number of registrants. A complementary hypothesis is that there is a relatively stable number of librarians in the profession who participate in continuing education courses at the national level. As more organizations are getting into the act of producing continuing education courses, the slice of the pie available to any one organization is likely to become progressively smaller. Preliminary data from SLA, MLA, ACRL, ASIS, and ARL suggest this trend.

These very preliminary data bear additional scrutiny and data gathering, but they are provocative for continuing education providers. In order to grow our programs, we need to increase the number of people participating in continuing education, encourage those who are already enrolling to take more courses, and to rethink our delivery systems and change our formats.

What other things have we learned that should impact on our future programming? It was mentioned earlier in this paper that research has shown that some library staff receive more support to go to conferences than to attend independently held continuing education courses. Salaries received by the large majority of library staffs are not sufficient to support expensive continuing education activities when such activities are not paid for by the employing institution. And we know that well planned formal continuing education activities, which provide continuous feedback to participants, are relatively expensive.

We are experiencing a tightening job market which comes as a result of budgetary cuts affecting libraries and an extension of the mandatory retirement age from sixty-five to seventy years. The tightened job market has resulted in less job mobility as people choose the security of existing employment, and there are fewer job openings for those who do wish to make a change.

There is an increasing awareness of self-responsibility for professional development. As career opportunities become increasingly competitive it is in the individual's self-interest to have maintained currency and even demonstrably to have contributed to the profession through formal professional development activities, participation in association activities, committee membership, and publication.

With less turnover among library staffs, employers will need to find ways of stimulating and renewing their library staffs through internally-developed opportunities. At the same time we will continue to be faced with limited resources for such development. As a result we will need to look for more home-grown varieties of continuing education opportunities. Examples we are beginning to see more of include:

—brief reassignment to other positions either within the library or to other libraries;
—regular rotation during the first years of beginning appointments;
—assignments to committees within the library;
—assignment to problem-solving task forces;
—visits to other libraries;
—in-house staff development programming, such as each unit taking responsibility for a mini-update of advances in their field; and
—exchange programs with counterparts in other libraries, even in other countries.

Since many people find that their most meaningful professional learning experience comes as a result of dealing with an on-the-job challenge, we need to develop opportunities that promote problem solving. The establishment of task forces within a library has already been mentioned. Social interaction with colleagues can provide an environment for informal problem solving or for discussing issues of mutual concern. Librarians should deliberately plan occasions when such informal exchange can take place and recognize the benefit of this type of activity. This type of learning experience also points to the need of the librarian to recognize and respond to his/her own need at an individually-motivated level.

If it is so that employers are more supportive of employees attending professional meetings than separately held continuing education courses, then groups conducting meetings should perhaps try to conduct continuing education courses in conjunction with professional meetings. In this way they will hit a captive audience whose expenses are more likely to have been paid.

For whatever reasons, librarians are often unwilling to pay the real cost of continuing education programming. In order to have formally planned experiences at low cost, it will be necessary to design continuing education programming at the local level by largely volunteer groups. In this way a significant part of the cost of programming can be split up and borne *invisibly* by the individuals and their employing institutions. Continuing education programming carried out by a paid staff, and having to recover all staff and operating costs, results in a high cost per participant.

If the preliminary data we have from the Medical Library Association, the Special Libraries Association, the American Society for Information Science, and the Association of College and Research Libraries stands up to further testing, they may indicate that we have reached a saturated market for formal continuing education programs. This does not mean that these organizations should decrease their activity, but rather assess:

1. What it will cost them to attract further participants.
2. Why potential participants are interested in continuing education and what that knowledge might mean for designing alternate forms of continuing education.
3. What other delivery mechanism for continuing education should be pursued and made cost-effective.
4. How to design continuing education opportunities that can be used by local groups and libraries at the grass roots level.

There is a place for the development and offering of quality formal continuing education courses. A national association, because it is national in scope, has the opportunity to repeat courses for its membership in various parts of the country, as well as in conjunction with its national conference.

For the individual, the need for continuous self-development will be necessary for survival in the profession. Developments are taking place daily which change the library and the delivery of information services. There are other librarians coming up through the ranks who are eager for our slots if we are perceived to be marking time or resistant to change. As times get tougher for libraries, and they will, employers will be unable to afford staff who are viewed as "not pulling their weight."

For those librarians working in smaller libraries, where it is difficult to get time off because there is no one to cover the position, there is often a compounding sense of isolation and of being away from the mainstream of current advances. Without a broad peer group of support and interaction, the need for association with colleagues is even more important. The responsibility to set up structures to get that peer reinforcement is again the individuals. The association's responsibility is to suggest structures that people in these situations might try, and to develop products and services that can reach people at their home level.

Challenges and Constraints Facing Associations

Taking the foregoing into account, I would include the following as specific challenges facing associations in their role of developing professional competency.

Development of Specific Competency Data

The King study, in as far as it will go, will provide a useful set of data about required competencies. Yet the data identified will only be the tip of the iceberg. As Griffiths said in her talk on Sunday evening: "Once the competencies are set out, it is the role of the schools and the professional societies to redefine them and to provide the training." From her figure 2, one can see that the King study will stop at the level of the first wide bar—i.e., the "identification, definition, description, and validation of competencies." It will be the library associations or schools which will have to design and implement competency attainment measures and evaluate them for validity and reliability. And to do so will require much greater specificity in the definition of the competencies.

From my experiences in developing the competencies used in the Medical Library Association's certification examination, I know that this is a difficult, expensive, and very large next step. Yet it is an essential one, not only for basic education and certification purposes, but as a necessary next step to developing self-assessment tools that individuals can use to plug into professional development programs. It is not enough to know you need "management skills"—rather one needs to know exactly what skills and at what level.

The financial costs of going this next step are too great to be borne by any one institution and will likely have to be borne by an association, a grant, or some combination of the two.

Costs of Developing Model Programs

One of the roles previously described is to develop highly visible models of "good" or innovative service to demonstrate both to the profession and to our outside audiences ways in which libraries effectively support society, institutions or businesses in situations that may be different from stereotypical librarians' roles. Yet such activities cost money to be successful. For example, the Medical Library Association film cost $85,000 in today's market. The Bibliographic Instruction Liaison Project of ACRL has cost $50,000. In both these instances the dollars came from membership dues and other revenue sources. These funds are increasingly being eaten up by the basic operating costs of the associations—as inflation has outpaced membership, dues increase.

The Stereotypes and Realities of the Profession

To some extent we are caught in the chicken and the egg syndrome. When I used to show medical directors and administrators the file "Rx: Information" they would become excited about the prospect of what their hospital library could become—an integral, throbbing part of the patient care team. Inevitably they would turn to me and say, "find me a librarian like that" and I could not. For reasons of low pay, unattractiveness as a dynamic stimulating profession, lack of job mobility or what have you, librarianship does not always attract the kind of people we like to think we are.

As one participant at this conference said during a coffee break, "they blame the library schools for what we turn out and say we should be more selective—they should see what we get to work with from the start." This is a very real problem which has to be addressed.

Too Narrow a Definition of Continuing Education

In assisting librarians in maintaining their professional competence we need to overcome the perception that continuing education is achieved by short courses only. The opportunities for continuing education are limited only by our imagination and creativity. Continuing education is *anything* that helps a person or institution do something better, learn something new, or think about something in a different way. It includes:

—attending state and local library meetings, or conferences;
—visiting exhibits or suppliers/vendors;
—establishing journal clubs or sharing journal subscriptions;
—reading library journals, books or reports on your own;
—looking at the advertisements in library journals;
—preparing a talk or a course;
—listening to an audiocassette or viewing a videocassette;
—writing a paper;
—taking a self-study course;
—reading news items about library programs elsewhere, and thinking about how to adapt them to your own library situation;
—working on a committee or task force; and
—solving a problem at work, or talking with a colleague about library related matters.

Inability to Assume Responsibility for Professional Development

Some librarians fail to recognize that, while it is nice for an employer to support one's efforts to maintain and improve professional competence, the lack of such support does not absolve the employee of this self-responsibility. It may require the librarian to seek less expensive ways of maintaining old, and developing new, competencies.

Continuing Education and Other Forms of
Professional Development Should Not Cost Much

The belief that continuing education programming, conferences, workshops, association memberships, etc. should not cost very much is an unrealistic view, perhaps encouraged by an extension of the view of a library as a public good. The reality is that these forms of maintaining professional competence have to be funded from somewhere. Association members can be heard to complain that a workshop costs $100 a day, or that their membership dues cost $75 or $100 a year. When it comes to formal programming you get what you pay for, or someone else has picked up a lot of hidden costs. Quality programming costs money.

Directions for Future Association Efforts

Associations will continue to play many of the key roles in developing professional competence as they have in the past. These roles will include the holding of national and local meetings, promoting exhibits, publishing journals and other materials, promulgating standards of performance, sponsoring courses and institutes, monitoring educational requirements, and publicizing the profession.

Over the next several years increased emphasis is likely to be placed on the following roles:

1. A reexamination of the basic education for librarianship and information science. In this process attention will need to be given to such thorny issues as:
   —The minimum size of a library school for it to maintain a large enough critical mass to exist.
   —The possible dissolution of schools that cannot adapt to a changing environment.
   —A greater accountability on the part of the schools for the students they graduate.
2. In turn, the profession, probably through the associations, will need to focus on what the profession sees as needed competencies. Competencies, in much greater detail than those developed by the King project, will be developed to help guide library education curricula, self-

assessment, and continuing education programming. And once developed, they will need to be monitored and updated regularly.

3. The associations, together with the library schools, have an important role to play in promoting the concept of lifelong learning as a part of professional responsibility. The associations have a special responsibility to inculcate this viewpoint into the minds of employing institutions, as a routine cost of doing business.

4. Associations will continue to be exploring mechanisms for cost-effective delivery systems for professional development. This will include assistance with programming at the local level as well as the delivery of national programs through audio and video teleconferencing.

5. Associations need to monitor and publicize trends in the profession, the economy and society to bring them to the attention of members so that these members are not caught unawares. The associations need to concentrate on developing credibility so that these early warning signals will not go unheeded.

6. A final role for which the effective association will plan, is that of promoter of librarianship to the many audiences with whom libraries and librarians come in contact. This will be a marketing task in the sense of the word "marketing" as Ted Leavitt meant it to be used. From each of our audiences we will identify what needs and wants the library can fill for them, and then respond in those terms:

   —For the hospital administrator we can promote the concept of the librarian as contributing to better patient care.

   —For the politician the library can represent a better satisfied constituency.

   —For the management consulting and executive search firm the librarian can be the reassurance that a fast library search has resulted in a carefully researched project proposal that will not be an embarrassment because a recent relevant article was not referred to in it.

   —For the potential library school student, the library must be projected as a dynamic, challenging institution.

   —For the college president the library, through its bibliographic instruction programs, can represent a superior educational resource.

   —For the student the library represents the security of knowing a book or article is accessible through the reserve book room.

   —To regional accrediting agencies, the library symbolizes a commitment to knowledge and learning.

As a marketing *and* public relations agency the associations can help shape the role that future libraries and librarians will play in our society.

One final note. Associations play many roles in the furtherance of the profession and in developing professional competence. However, an association is not a discrete body—it is you, the people, working together, that create any role at all.

REFERENCES

1. Carr-Saunders, A.M., and Wilson, P.A. "Professions." *Encyclopaedia of the Social Sciences*, vol. 12, edited by Edwin R.A. Seligman, et al., p. 476. New York: MacMillan Co., 1934.

2. Lanier, Don. "Invoking Our Standards." *Wilson Library Bulletin* 57(Jan. 1983):373.

3. Virgo, Julie A., et al. *Continuing Education Needs Assessment and Model Programs.* Washington, D.C.: CLENE, 1977, p. 80.

4. Conroy, Barbara. *Library Staff Development and Continuing Education: Principles and Practices.* Littleton, Colo.: Libraries Unlimited, 1978, pp. xiii-xiv.

5. Flowers, Janet L. "Role of the Local Professional Association in Continuing Education." *College & Research Libraries News* 41(July/Aug. 1980):99.

6. Wagner, Mary M., and Mahmoodi, Suzanne H. "Continuing Education Needs of Minnesota Library/Information Center/Media Center Personnel." *Minnesota Libraries* 26(Winter 1979/80):526; Virgo, *Continuing Education Needs Assessment;* and Neal, James G. "Continuing Education: Attitudes and Experiences of the Academic Librarian." *College & Research Libraries* 41(March 1980):130. (As quoted in Stone, Elizabeth W. *Factors Related to the Professional Development of Librarians.* Metuchen, N.J.: Scarecrow Press, 1969, p. 209.)

7. Neal, "Continuing Education," p. 130.

8. Ibid., p. 132.

9. Ibid., p. 131.

10. Martin, Allie Beth, and Dugan, Maryann. *Continuing Education for Library Staffs in the Southwest: A Survey and Recommendations.* Dallas, Texas: Southwestern Library Association, 1974, p. 31.

11. Virgo, et al., *Continuing Education Needs Assessment.*

12. Schwedes, Jeffrey T., ed. "Libraries Polled on Travel Policies." *College & Research Libraries News* 41(July/Aug. 1980):195.

13. Neal, "Continuing Education."

14. Virgo, et al., *Continuing Education Needs Assessment.*

JO AN S. SEGAL
Executive Director
Bibliographical Center for Research

Competencies for Library Networking and Cooperation

Since Sunday evening we have enjoyed outstanding papers on the competencies required for the use of the new information technologies in librarianship. We have looked at the needs for using technology, the kinds of competencies needed in different types of libraries, and training and education needed for developing these competencies. The final section of the program has included Julie Virgo's paper on the association role in developing professional competence. I would like to present an argument which I hope will both offer some new material and provide a framework for summarizing many of the ideas presented during the course of the clinic. I will discuss competencies needed by librarians from the point of view of the cooperative library agency. I see two major needs.

The first is for a body of professionals to work in such agencies and the second is for an enlightened clientele of librarians who are familiar with the role of those agencies and able to take the greatest advantage of what they can offer. I believe that the secret of these competencies lie less in knowing how to perform certain tasks than in a values clarification process which identifies values such as cooperation, humanism and ethical behavior as foremost among the characteristics needed by librarians in cooperating for the use of library technology.

COMPETENCIES FOR LIBRARIANS WORKING IN NETWORKS, CONSORTIA, OR SYSTEMS

The major areas of competency which I believe are necessary for librarians who wish to work in cooperative agencies of one kind or another fall in seven categories. The first is communication theory and practice; the second, teaching and training competencies; the third, mastery of the field of librarianship; the fourth, knowledge of specific systems which form the basis for the service of the agency; fifth, business administration; sixth, planning ability and skills. The seventh "competency" is not really a competency at all but a clarification of values.

Communication Theory and Practice

The librarian wishing to work in a networking situation must have some understanding of communication theory and practice. Topics which should be familiar to such librarians include a knowledge of group dynamics and how a group functions and what the relationships are between people and how they can best be recognized and used to facilitate the work of the group.

A second skill is in the area of interpersonal relations. It is important that network librarians understand the dynamics of interpersonal relationships in their work with each other and with the staffs of the libraries whom they are serving.

A third skill is that of organizational communication; the ability to assist member libraries in evaluating the communication which goes on in the library and in facilitating the work flow is extremely important. This knowledge needs to be practiced within the network as well.

A fourth extremely important ability of network librarians is that they must possess good listening skills. We think that we are good listeners but in fact we are usually politely, or less politely, awaiting our turn in a conversation. The ability to hear what other people are saying and what feelings are imbedded in what they are saying is extremely important.

The next communication skill is one usually included in job descriptions—that of writing and editing. The network librarian is expected to be able to express him- or herself competently in writing. This is an extremely important skill, particularly as we are required to provide documentation for systems which are not always easy to use and for which inadequate documentation is often provided by the system designers. Editing of our own and one another's work is also part of this activity.

Finally, we must be able to express ourselves orally. Network librarians are constantly being called upon to make public comments. Whether we are speaking extemporaneously before a meeting where we happen to be the only one who has any information about a certain topic, or whether we have been asked to provide a formal paper at a meeting such as this conference, public speaking is a skill which network librarians will be called upon to practice.

Teaching and Training

Since continuing education activities are a large part of the work of networks, consortia, etc., the capacity to teach or train is an extremely important skill needed by network librarians. In order to decide what kinds of training to offer, networks must evaluate the need. Needs assessment activities are highly important and skill in this area can be acquired.

Second, the network librarian needs to be able to prepare and carry out workshops and training sessions. Skills needed for this activity are administrative, teaching and documentation skills. All of these are extremely important and none can be slighted. It may be that different combinations of staff are needed to carry out all the functions, but the more versatile the individual librarians are, the better will be the quality of the workshops or training offered by the network.

Next, the network librarian must be able to design the instruction itself. This requires a broad knowledge of the field of librarianship plus a knowledge of the specific area for training and teaching, and finally an understanding of instructional methodology for teaching adults. Adult education techniques differ from pedagogical techniques and include more enlightened use of audiovisual materials, group participation methods, a constant gauging of reactions, and fast on-the-feet thinking about potential new directions the training must take.

Finally, in order to provide a well-rounded teaching and training program, the network must select personnel from inside the staff and from external sources. Knowing what one's shortcomings are is an important part of this effort. The careful selection of an outside consultant may enhance the network's ability to serve its libraries far beyond the short-term economics of providing training with in-house staff.

Mastery of the Field of Librarianship

Network librarians must have a broad mastery of the field of librarianship. It is unwise to choose for network staff the person who has limited experience. The most valuable network staff will include individuals who have served in different types of libraries, in both technical and public services, and in both practical and academic aspects of librarianship. This mix of staff will lead to credibility of the staff in the eyes of librarians in specific types and sizes of libraries, and in both public and technical services, and will thereby increase the network's effectiveness in dealing with its publics.

In order to keep abreast of what is occurring, networks must encourage and support their staff in their attendance at conferences and membership in professional associations and must provide a decent professional collection for their regular use. No network librarian can afford not to meet regularly with his or her colleagues, or not to keep in touch with the journals which carry information about library cooperation and technology, and the major conferences on library cooperation and technology that go on.

Knowledge of Specific Systems

Next comes a competency which probably is the first one that would jump to many individuals' minds in thinking of what a person would need in order to be a competent network librarian—namely, knowledge of the specific systems which form the basis for the service the agency provides.

Cooperative agencies include those which offer interlibrary loan services, those which provide technical processing for groups of libraries, those which provide online database searching, those which offer cooperative purchasing, those which exist for the purpose of collection development, and those which provide OCLC or other bibliographic utilities as their main product and service. Many networks provide combinations of these products and services. While individual staff members in networks may specialize in one or another of these systems, it is advisable that everyone on the staff have some knowledge of all the systems. This is important whether you are representing the network at a State Library Conference, making a speech, attending a professional meeting, or answering the telephone when the person in charge of that department happens to be out of town. This knowledge of systems can only be kept up through constant use of the systems.

While several suggestions for this kind of competency maintenance have been made, few networks have adequately solved the problem of providing opportunities for use of systems by their staff. Some ideas for improving this situation include: exchanges of staff between libraries and networks, undertaking of specific projects for libraries so that staff librarians will have the opportunity to practice systems operation, and repeated attendance at advanced training workshops especially designed for network staffs.

Business Administration

Networks are not libraries. Some of them are governmentally supported but many more than half of the twenty-two OCLC networks are not-for-profit corporations which operate very much like small businesses. As the BCR Board likes to point out, we are a not-for-profit corporation but we are also not-for-loss. Four areas which need to be attended to in the area of business administration are: financial literacy, personnel management, library management, and the care and nurturing of governance boards.

Network librarians often arrive on the scene with very little knowledge of finance. Simply being able to read a balance sheet and understand what it says is extremely important. This knowledge must be within the competencies of the network administrators, but the more knowledge there is among the staff of the agency as to the detailed financial affairs of the agency, the better run it will be. This is important because staff members must understand what the network's financial position is, why prices are set the way they are, and what leeway a network has in charging or not charging for its services in order to deal with libraries. In the area of personnel management, the usual skills for hiring and firing and for maintaining a motivated and satisfied staff are complicated by the fact that the agency is constantly represented outside its walls by its employees. Any dissatisfaction felt by those employees will be communicated to those with whom they come in contact regularly. The importance of keeping one's house in order, therefore, extends outside the walls of the institution.

Another sensitive matter is that network staffs are required to travel a great deal. This causes a kind of stress on the staff and on the relationships among staff members in an agency, which only those who have worked in settings where there is a great deal of staff travel can understand. Staff members return from trips with their briefcases loaded with tasks they have promised to perform for the librarians they have just left. When they arrive in the office they find their desks piled high with work which did not cease to come in just because they were on the road. Besides that, everyone seems to need to see them that day as soon as possible, and telephone calls are lined up waiting for them to answer. This causes enough stress in and of itself, but it also happens at a moment when they have been unable to speak to other staff members and they may feel that they have lost touch with what has been going on in the office during their absence. The management of personnel in this environment is at best difficult; a great deal of skill must be exercised in order to prevent serious burn-out and other personnel problems.

In the area of library management, network staff are frequently called upon to make recommendations regarding work flow. They are expected to know several different kinds of systems and to be able to make comparisons between them and to keep a somewhat objective point of view regarding this, whether or not they represent one major system. They may be called upon to make suggestions regarding the planning of space. All of these activities require that they acquire these competencies and share them with one another.

Finally, all networks have some kind of governing board. In most instances, this board is elected in whole or in part directly by the membership, and serves as the ultimate authority over the executive director and the staff of the agency. Working with a governance board is a challenge and a skill which can be developed. Few courses in this aspect of management are offered. A thorough understanding of the difference between governance and management needs to be instilled in a governance board; however, the limits to management's authority need to be taken into account by every chief executive officer.

Planning Ability and Skills

It would be impossible to say too much about the need for planning in the running of a library networking agency. Both short-term tactical planning and long-range strategic planning must be carried out by the network staff. In this regard, it should be pointed out that governance bodies play an extremely important role, although they must have competent advice from the network staff. This advice will only be valuable if it is based on a thorough grounding in economic, political and library technology trends, coupled with a thorough understanding of the organization's role and mission and the specific needs and desires of the libraries involved in the organization.

Values Clarification

Finally, a "competency" which is not a competency involves the clarification of a set of values for library network agency staff which must override all other considerations. The values of cooperation, of ethical behavior, and of human versus machine superiority must be examined and espoused by network staff if their efforts are to be seen as valid and credible. Espousing the cause of library cooperation while acting in an extremely competitive fashion with other networks or consortia, for example, is intrinsically contradictory and may reduce the credibility of an agency. Behaving ethically requires attention to both professional and business dealings between network librarians and library users.

Finally, in a profession which has long emphasized humanistic values, a network stands in danger of being seen as espousing technology at the expense of humans. Clarifying where one's values are is very important in order to maintain the credibility necessary to work in the world of librarians.

COMPETENCIES FOR LIBRARIANS IN GENERAL

In addition to competencies needed by librarians who wish to work in networks, I see a whole set of competencies necessary for librarians in order to make them effective users of networks and of library technology, particularly in the aspects of library technology which are cooperative in nature. In this area I see six major competencies which I would like to address. They are a broad view of librarianship, acceptance of responsibility for the profession as a whole, a cooperative attitude, openness to new modes of interaction, values clarification, and a knowledge of technology.

Broad View of Librarianship

This is less a competency than an attitude. It includes a willingness to continue learning through courses, workshops, training sessions, keeping up with the literature, and belonging to professional associations. It supposes an interest in librarianship which extends outside one's own library and outside one's own specialty.

Acceptance of Responsibility for the Profession as a Whole

This includes working with other librarians toward mutual goals. It means being active in professional associations and in the community as a spokesperson for librarianship and information science. Finally, it means being willing to seek cooperative solutions to common problems.

Cooperative Attitude

This attitude will be expressed in a willingness to seek solutions outside the usual framework of the zero-sum game. This means looking for a way to solve problems where all parties can come out ahead: no mean task. It also underlies a kind of generosity which urges a librarian to give his/her own time or to allow subordinates to use work time for cooperative projects.

Openness to New Modes of Interacting

This, again, is an attitude. It involves being open to treating vendors as something other than "the enemy," and recognizing that other types of libraries are neither "snooty" nor "inferior," but that all libraries have their own special needs while sharing certain commonalities. It means regarding networks and other cooperative agencies as friends wanting to help libraries; courting publishers and allowing them to court you—and accepting their concerns about copyright. Finally, it means learning to overcome natural fears about technology by learning to use it for our own purposes.

Values Clarification

The same principles mentioned as desirable for network librarians apply here, too. Librarians need to clarify their attitudes about cooperation and autonomy. They need to be aware of the ethical problems associated with the automation of information, and they need to apply the principles of the ALA Code of Ethics to the unfamiliar areas of computers and databases. They must also consider the role of the new technology in their familiar library world. Where do computers fit in? How should they be harnessed to serve the cause of libraries and library users?

Knowledge of Technology

Lastly, the librarian needs to become competent in technology. Only in this way can its advantages be used to increase library effectiveness and efficiency.

SUMMARY

From the networking point of view, we need professionals to work in networks, and librarians to work with them. The advent of widespread library automation fosters a need to clarify the values of professional librarianship. In relation to "networking," I believe in the values of cooperation, humanism, and ethical behavior. These are less competencies than attitudes, but they can be learned and I believe library educators, library administrators, and other influential librarians can and should espouse these values as exemplary.

CONTRIBUTORS

LINDA BASKIN is Computer Coordinator for the Illinois Cooperative Extension Service and is responsible for development of a statewide network of microcomputers. In addition to general computer awareness, she has introduced staff to word processing, database systems, software development, and other microcomputer applications. Ms. Baskin has also been involved in developing software for the IBM personal computer, Apple and PLATO.

EVELYN H. DANIEL is Dean and Professor, School of Information Studies, Syracuse University. She holds a Ph.D. in Library and Information Science from the University of Maryland and has taught at the University of Kentucky and the University of Rhode Island prior to joining the faculty at Syracuse in 1976. She served as Coordinator of the Consortium for Developing Competency-Based Education Program for Media Specialists and her publications include her report *A Process for Developing a Competency-Based Educational Program for Media Professionals.*

CAROLYN M. GRAY is Assistant Director for Technical Services and Automation at Brandeis University Library in Waltham, Massachusetts. She holds an M.L.S. from the University of Oklahoma and her previous positions include Head of Cataloging and Coordinator of Automation at Western Illinois University and Assistant to the Director of the AMIGOS Bibliographic Council where she did training for several online systems. She has served as President of the Library & Information Technology Association, a division of the American Library Association.

HILLIS L. GRIFFIN is Director of the Technical Information Services Department at Argonne National Laboratory in Illinois. He holds an M.L.S. from the University of Washington and has been at Argonne since 1962 when he was appointed to be information systems librarian. His responsibilities at Argonne have included the development and implementation of automated systems in support of library operations, including the specification and selection of appropriate equipment. He has taught courses on library automation for the University of Illinois, the University of Wisconsin, and Rosary College.

JOSÉ-MARIE GRIFFITHS is Vice President of King Research, Inc. She has a Ph.D. in Information Science from University College London and has recently completed studies concerning the incorporation of new technology into library and information system operations for the U.S.

Geological Survey, State of North Carolina, Department of Energy, and U.S. Army. She is the author of a text entitled *Application of Minicomputers and Microcomputers to Information Handling* recently published by Unesco and has presented several seminars and courses dealing with new technology in both the United States and the United Kingdom.

KATHRYN LUTHER HENDERSON is Associate Professor in the Graduate School of Library and Information Science at the University of Illinois at Urbana-Champaign, where she teaches courses related to cataloging and classification, bibliographic organization and control, and technical services. Prior to her present position she served as a cataloger in theological seminary and university libraries. Her major publication and research efforts are related to the history of descriptive cataloging. She has edited volumes related to *Trends in American Publishing, MARC Uses and Users,* and *Major Classification Systems: the Dewey Centennial* and served as the coeditor of *Conserving and Preserving Library Materials.* She was one of the first persons to have developed computer-assisted instruction for library science students.

DANUTA A. NITECKI is Associate Director for Public Services, University of Maryland Libraries. She has an M.S. in Library Science from Drexel University and an M.S. in Communications from the University of Tennessee, Knoxville. Her previous positions include coordinator, Illinois Research & Reference Activities in the University of Illinois at Urbana-Champaign Library and head, Interlibrary Services Department and Coordinator of Automated Information Retrieval Services in the University of Tennessee Library. She has served as president of the Reference & Adult Services Division (RASD) of the American Library Association and has contributed to *RQ* both as the editor of the column "Online Services" and as database reviews editor.

JO AN S. SEGAL is Executive Director of the Bibliographical Center for Research (BCR) in Denver, Colorado. She holds a Ph.D. in communication from the University of Colorado and an M.S. in Library Science from Columbia University. Prior to joining BCR in 1978, she served for six years as librarian for the Western Interstate Commision for Higher Education. She served as chairman of the Special Libraries Association's Education Division in 1981-82 and is the author of papers on adult and lifelong learning.

LINDA C. SMITH is Associate Professor in the Graduate School of Library and Information Science at the University of Illinois at Urbana-

Champaign. She received a Ph.D. from the School of Information Studies at Syracuse University. Her fields of interest include information retrieval, library automation and science reference service.

MIMA SPENCER is Associate Director of the ERIC Clearinghouse on Elementary and Early Childhood Education at the University of Illinois at Urbana-Champaign. In recent years, she has presented workshops on computer literacy to educators and information specialists and has been involved in software design, staff training for file building and word processing, computer conferencing, and bibliographic searching.

RICHARD T. SWEENEY is Executive Director of the Public Library of Columbus & Franklin County in Columbus, Ohio. He holds an M.L.S. in Library and Information Science from Drexel University and served as Director of both the Genesee County (Michigan) Public Library and of the Atlantic City Free Public Library prior to coming to Columbus in 1979. He currently serves as President of Columbus Community Cable Access, Inc. and has authored articles on remote electronic delivery of information through libraries.

JULIE CARROLL VIRGO is Executive Director of the Association of College and Research Libraries (ACRL), American Library Association. She holds a Ph.D. in Librarianship from the University of Chicago and served as Director of Education for the Medical Library Association for a five year period before taking her present position in 1977. She is an active member of several professional associations and is the author of papers on various aspects of library education and professional continuing education.

INDEX